Faith

THE WUHAN INCIDENT

Mark Fulmer

THE
WUHAN
INCIDENT

BIOWEAPONS AND THE
EMERGING GLOBAL RESET

Mark Fulmer

LIBERTY HILL ELITE

Liberty Hill Publishing
2301 Lucien Way #415
Maitland, FL 32751
407.339.4217
www.libertyhillpublishing.com

Paperback ISBN-13: 978-1-6628-4879-7
Ebook ISBN-13: 978-1-6628-4881-0

TABLE OF CONTENTS

PREFACE

I n December of 2019 at Kansas City International Airport, I was getting ready to board a flight home after spending the Christmas hol-
idays with my wife's family when a particular news story being aired
on the television monitor in the terminal waiting area caught my eye:
Mysterious Disease Outbreak in China. The news anchor discussed
the strange respiratory illness during growing speculation to whether
it could be either some new strain of avian influenza or even another
occurrence of SARS. I did not realize at the time that this was the pre-
cursor to what would be eventually called *Coronavirus* which made
such a global impact that life in 2020 would be disrupted on every
continent politically, socially, and economically.

The news of this outbreak in China at that time seemed worlds
away as we began to hear of the number of new cases reported
everyday along with deaths caused by the mystery disease. It was
not until a couple of months later Sunday night on February 2, 2020,
while at a Superbowl party that my work mobile phone started to
light up with messages and calls just before half-time about an emergency conference call. I quickly diverted my attention from the Kansas
City Chiefs to the conference call with members of local emergency
management, elected officials, public health directors along with a
representative from the CDC who introduced himself as a quarantine station officer. We were told about an Asian flight that would
be arriving within the next twenty-four hours and that we needed to

activate isolation and quarantine protocols to limit potential spread of the Chinese virus to local populations.

At that time, there had been a few isolated occurrences with business travelers returning from Asian countries with the infection who had to be hospitalized, so there were obvious concerns about more travelers entering the U.S. On January 30th earlier that year, President Trump made the decision to restrict all flights from China as a matter of public safety which resulted in a great deal of criticism from his political opponents who called him "xenophobic" and that he was "fear-mongering." Trump was more than just erring on the side of caution at that time as he had the best interest of our national security and protection in mind given that infected travelers posed a great threat to our citizens. And what proved to be an even more daunting challenge for the nation's safety would be the millions of travelers, who although did not come directly from China, but had some secondary exposure to someone else who was in mainland China. Suddenly, everyone had to answer survey questions such as "Have you been out of the U.S? Have you had contact with someone from the Hubei province of China?" Temperature scans were implemented as routine practice.

Then in a matter of weeks, the nation moved quickly beyond just a few isolated cases to occurrences of what epidemiologists would call "community spread" that impacted every state in the nation. All of it seemed quite unreal at the time with the declaration made in March 2020 by the World Health Organization (WHO) and the Centers for Disease Control (CDC) that we were now in the midst of a global pandemic. Every day the media announced the number of COVID-19 deaths as we started to hear about federal and state mandates everywhere to wash our hands and to wear a mask in public. Only what was deemed as "critical infrastructure" was allowed to remain open as schools, businesses and even churches began to shut down.

The mood of the nation was not only somber but quite fearful as this strange apocalypse seemed to be spinning out of control. Not only was there news about a pandemic to contend with but within months there were incidents in major U.S. cities of civil unrest: rioting, looting, anarchy, and mass violence. Nearly every night the media would show scenes of major cities burning while we started to hear about demands for social justice and calls to defund the police. While most law-abiding citizens were inside their homes during mandated lockdowns, BLM and Antifa took to the streets to orchestrate violent mayhem in the name of public protests. Adding insult to injury, as most political conservatives were alarmed to see an increased attack on their freedoms, moral values, and constitutional rights as the year ended with the outcome of a disappointing national election. It seemed as if the hopes of a strong constitutional republic were being dashed. Social media giants began to systematically mass censor any opinions contrary to the party line and agenda of the left with an outright attack on free speech. An extreme movement of political correctness emerged overnight with little or zero tolerance for conservative ideas. All of this came within months of a declaration of a global pandemic.

The year 2020 and the earlier part of 2021 with the COVID-19 pandemic was a perfect storm packaged in global crisis with all the making of an Orwellian 1984 novel – "Big Brother" as government implemented over-reaching controls over businesses and churches nearly everywhere. Small business owners were fined for operating during closures, and even pastors of churches were arrested for defying orders for their churches to remain closed despite apparent contradictions that "big-box" stores could remain open. Everywhere we started seeing signs on public buildings that were limited to fifty percent or less occupancy stating that masks were required for entry. Once inside these buildings, we had to maintain social distancing minimums of six feet.

Further into 2021, there were many questions being raised by citizens regarding not only the origins of this pandemic but the so-called scientific data that dictated government policies for restrictive closures and medical treatment. Why were discussions being shut down on social media regarding alternative treatments such as hydroxychloroquine and Ivermectin? Contradictory guidance about the wearing of masks was not only confusing but misleading (i.e., one mask or two masks?). We need not only to pursue the answers to these questions but to also search for the truth aggressively. American patriots must pick up the gauntlet for this generation, and the next, to seek answers in the aftermath of this pandemic. The integrity of our republic hangs in the balance.

INTRODUCTION

I f your first reaction to the initial COVID-19 crisis in early 2020 was that the world was quickly reeling out of control like being stuck on a run-away freight train with no way off for escape, you are not alone. Most of us were broadsided by the rapid progression of cata-strophic events brought on by the pandemic – loss of life, jobs, income and eventually loss of our individual rights and freedoms. Added to that, the social upheaval with civil unrest and mass rioting was like a "blitzkrieg" assault upon the very fabric of our constitutional republic. All of this seemed unreal like some sinister plot out of a Tom Clancy novel leaving us with the question: was this really a naturally occurring pandemic as claimed or was there something purely intentional that was developed with COVID-19? For that reason, some commentators have used the term "plan-demic" to question the natural origin of this disease. Is there a grand global conspiracy lurking in the shadows?

While there are many so called conspiracy theories that abound on the internet and social media regarding the origin of COVID, I have no interest in adding another fruitless speculation to the bone pile. My hope is to encourage constructive dialogue that may help us to begin the journey towards the truth. My first disclaimer is this: I do not have the answers, nor do I have any conclusive evidence regarding the origin or the intents of this pandemic. By the time this book is published there will be more books written along with investigative journalists who are joining this growing movement of those searching for answers. I am encouraged to see investigative journalists like Australia's Sharri Markson whose research team has conducted comprehensive research and interviews with dozens of subject matter experts – some of these sources I have provided for you in the appendix and bibliography.

Beginning with a look at what I call "COVID-19 Ground Zero" in Wuhan China, I propose the following hypothesis – that this virus could possibly be a biological weapon of mass destruction that was delivered with the intent of global disruption. I am not alone in putting forth such a hypothesis; there is an increasing number of researchers, virologists and experts from the scientific community that are bravely challenging the mainstream media narrative. To what end would be the purpose for creating (or manufacturing) a viral pathogen with the intent of world chaos? Whether it was an intentional or accidental viral release, I believe that it is possible that COVID was weaponized to deliberately create a world crisis. This crisis provided an excellent opportunity for the global elites such as George Soros and Bill Gates to launch their strategic plan for a global reset. That globalist sentiment is confidently expressed about the world-wide impact of the pandemic by Klaus Schwab, Chairman of the World Economic Forum: "A new world will emerge, the contours of which are for us to both imagine and to draw."[1]

Regardless of what conclusive evidence that emerges over the next few months and next few years concerning the Coronavirus, I am convinced that this pandemic has presented itself as a grand opportunity for the destructive forces of socialism and communism. These hostile forces on the left have weaponized the pandemic as a tool that threatens to undermine our freedoms and our constitutional republic. This is what I described earlier as the "blitzkrieg" assault that has gained momentum at the height of 2020. But for now, my hope is that American patriots will push back against this radical plan from socialist democrats and liberal media and call for investigations of the CDC, NIH, and WHO to arrive at the truth behind COVID.

---

[1] Klaus Schwab and Thierry Malleret, *COVID-19: The Great Reset*, (Geneva, Switzerland: Forum Publishing, 2020), 12.

The COVID bio-weapons hypothesis is a very serious one and should not be taken lightly. First and foremost, as an American patriot, I have a great concern for my country in these trying times. To substantiate such claims requires that a level of "reasonable credibility" be held by the author. Therefore, it is helpful to know about my background and experience to support my qualifications in the field of bioterrorism and emerging health threats. My twenty-year career began in public health epidemiology as a disease outbreak contact investigator. Just five years into my work in epidemiology I received an invitation from an individual who was working as a field supervisor in bioterrorism preparedness. They were familiar with my work as an epidemiology specialist and felt that with additional training my skills could be utilized to support their Biosecurity program. I was quickly launched into bioterrorism training to include chemical, biological, nuclear, and radiological weapons of mass destruction (CBRN WMD). Within twenty years, I advanced to being a senior planner and spent the last several years of my career in emergency preparedness management. In addition to serving as a subject matter expert on bioterrorism for local government councils, I have also been a guest lecturer in bioterrorism at local universities in North Texas.

While I do not lay claim to conclusive evidence that COVID's origin was a bioweapon, my research builds a case for a possible scenario that the virus was deliberately weaponized whether the initial release was accidental or intentional. I also offer some intriguing information on how the "emerging global reset" is exploiting the COVID outbreak to manufacture a crisis opportunity for big government and globalism to gain extensive control. Eventually one way or another we will find the truth about the origins of this pandemic; for the time being, we need to also understand the larger threat at hand that is far more dangerous than any viral pathogen – big government and globalist agendas that are seeking to undermine this constitutional republic and to take our long-cherished freedoms away (i.e., freedom of speech, election integrity, freedom of religion, traditional family values, our rights to a free capitalist enterprise, etc.).

All our God-given rights as American citizens are coming under assault by radical forces on the left, and they using the COVID crisis as an opportunity to do our republic harm while advancing their radical agendas. Although the residual effects of COVID will remain with us for a long time after the pandemic subsides, COVID will eventually fade away into the sunset and its usefulness as a tool to be sensationalized by the liberal media will also die out. After that, there will come another crisis which will be used as an opportunity to implement far reaching government control to threaten our freedom. Vice President Kamala Harris addressed the United Nations members in the spring of 2021 that international leaders need to begin preparing for the next global pandemic.[2] It is only a matter of time that the next crisis will occur providing another convenient opportunity for socialists and communists to seize power.

History has shown that neither socialism nor communism has any true compassion for human beings in crisis. Rather crises offer an opportunity to exploit the masses in order to implement radical change. This is exactly what Leni did during the great famines that struck the Volga region of Russia in the 1890's — he opposed any humanitarian assistance for the poor arguing that it was a convenient crisis to help collapse the local economy and to pave the way for socialism through revolution.[3] The "Great Reset" proposed by Schwab and other global elites follows the same template as Lenin's — use a global pandemic crisis as a means for "a new world to emerge." This is the greater threat we must be prepared for, the radical left's agenda to implement a "new world order" through global crisis.

---

[2] ABC News; *Harris tells UN body it's time to prepare for next pandemic*, Aamer Madhani, AP; April 26, 2021. Accessed June 28, 2021. https//abcnews.go.com/Politics/wireStory/harris-body-time-prep-pandemic-77315989

[3] Richard Pipes, *Communism: A History*. (New York, NY: Random House, 2003), 29.

CHAPTER 1

THE EASTERN DRAGON: THE CHINESE COMMUNIST PARTY

Universal human rights, democratic practice and the rule of law have powerful enemies, and China under the Chinese Communist Party is arguably the most formidable. The Party's program of influence and interference is well planned and bold and backed by enormous economic resources and technological power. – Clive Hamilton, Hidden Hand: How the Chinese Communist Party is Reshaping the World

The Need to Understand the Nature of the Threat Behind the Virus

The "main-stream" media would cringe every time that Donald Trump would make a reference to Coronavirus as the "China Virus." However, his brutal honesty was on target in more ways than one during a time when those within politically correct circles were reluctant to pin the geographic source of the virus's origin to China. Although shortly after the outbreak, it was no secret that the virus originated in mainland China, many were afraid either of offending diplomatic sensibilities or did not want to be labeled as "racist xenophobic' bigots." The reality is that COVID originated within one of the largest and most influential superpower nations on the face of the earth with a population of 1.4 billion and not in some remote sparsely populated jungle region. Given that the People's Republic of China is a modern industrialized nation with a gross domestic product value

1

of $14.1 trillion and not an impoverished third world country, it is reasonable to assume that we must consider the political and socio-economic construct of the nation where the virus originated. China is not merely a global superpower, but they are a brutal communist regime. While the Chinese people and its culture are both beautiful and amazing, they are under an oppressive totalitarian machine that strips them of any vestige of freedom and liberty. Millions of inno-cent Chinese men, women and children are victims of Communist oppression. It is no surprise any attempts at investigating the origins of COVID have been greatly obstructed by the Chinese Communist Party (CCP), which completely lacks any transparency and accountability. The machinery of communism is also a powerful tool in the hands of the global elites who are using the pandemic as an opportunity to seize control. Therefore, it will be helpful to look at the history of the CCP and the shaping of U.S. political policies and attitudes toward China as we undertake an investigation into the origins of the virus.

Communism – A Brief History

Karl Marx and Friedrich Engels developed their theory of political socialism within a philosophical context that promoted the idea of the equality of the classes. To promote this claim, they utilized methodology from natural sciences which had gained tremendous popularity among academics in the early nineteenth century. Marx and Engels formulated a doctrine of "scientific socialism which asserted that the ideal of a prop-ertyless, egalitarian society was something that not only should happen but, by virtue of the natural evolution of the economy, had to happen."[4] This concept of social evolution was directly influenced by Darwin's *On the Origin of the Species* written in 1859. Although Marx claimed to be objective in scientific methodology, his theories comprised a rigid and intolerant dogma that quickly dismissed any ideas contrary to his own.

---

[4] Richard Pipes, *Communism: A History* (New York: The Modern Library, 2003), 9

It should come as no surprise why the left is highly intolerant of any narrative that does not fit their own and why they weaponize misinformation when we look at Marxism. As Marx aggressively promoted his ideology, he defended his confrontation with anyone who disagreed with his narrative by stating: "criticism is not a scalpel but a weapon. Its object is the enemy [whom] it wishes not to refute but to destroy." The views of Marx and Engels expressed in their work *Das Kapital* were quite hostile to capitalism and free enterprise as they favored the redistribution of wealth in society.

Whereas the foundation for socialism had been developed by Marx and Engels at least in theory it was not until more militant leaders would emerge under the principles of the *Communist Manifesto* who advocated revolution after the First World War to crush capitalism and the bourgeoisie to liberate the working class. Lenin rose to the occasion to lead the Bolsheviks in Russia in November 1917. This revolution was bloody and brutal as Lenin's means of coercion came through a dictatorship. He believed that violent force was the means necessary to cease power by unleashing a civil war in Russia that claimed millions of lives. By 1924, a one-party state had formed that was a merger with Soviet Russia with its headquarters in Moscow. However, the new Communist State in Russia had to contend with economic disaster as there were food shortages. One of the worst famines in Russian devastated the nation claiming the lives of 5.2 million. Lenin had little compassion upon his own people and declared war on the rural population using force to take any remaining food to feed the Red Army. The famine became a convenient crisis that provided opportunity to further Lenin's revolution as those who were weakened by poverty and mass food shortages could offer very little resistance.

Lenin and his followers were determined to spread the revolution to the modern industrialized nations of the world: "We have emphasized that one cannot achieve such a task as a socialist revolution in one country. We knew that our victory will be a lasting victory only when our undertaking will conquer the whole world, because we had launched it exclusively counting on the world revolution."[5] The vision of communism became one of global conquest and was adopted by leaders such as Stalin who would promote a five-year economic plan in 1929 to industrialize their war machine through a rigorous government management of all production and all capital goods to include steel, iron, coal, oil and heavy machinery. Whereas Lenin failed to advance such bold economic causes, Stalin utilized a Marxist-Leninist axiom to build a labor state. Generations of Russians would barely subsist on meager wages to support the Communist State. Peasants were gathered into collective farms to labor for the benefit of the state as all their belongings were confiscated. Those who resisted were deported to labor camps in Siberian exile or even executed. This would become the *modus operandi* of communist nations around the world.

Mao's Gate of Heavenly Peace

我們偉大勝利的旗幟毛澤東和斯大木

Stalin in his vision to expand Communism's global conquest looked south to mainland China to recruit new revolutionaries. Mao Zedong was a devoted disciple of Stalin who grew up in a peasant family in the Hunan province. Mao was impressed by the Russian revolution and became an avid student of communism and soon enlisted as a young Marxist militant. His Communist regime set forth an aggressive campaign to transform Chinese society following in the footsteps of Lenin and Stalin. Stalin supplied Mao's soldiers with a massive number of arms and ammunition for the People's Liberation Army (PLA) to declare war on Chinese nationalists.

---

[5] Pipes, *Communism*, 49.

Mao fought his way to Beijing and on October 1, 1949, just a mere thirty-two years after the Russian Revolution, he and his soldiers climbed the historical Gate of Heavenly Peace (Tiananmen) in Beijing to announce victory.[6] The PLA eventually resisted the Japanese occupation of the Second World War and ruthlessly challenged any other foreign occupation. In a few years under Mao's leadership the People's Republic of China would rise as a seemingly invincible Communist nation.

Following a page out of Stalin's playbook, Mao established a brutal regime by executing millions and deporting those who resisted to labor camps. Land and property were confiscated for the cause of the state. By the 1950's, there were over 9.6 million detainees in hard labor camps and Communist party membership had grown to over 5.8 million who were loyal followers of Mao that were taught a song as children: *Communism is heaven, the commune is the ladder, if we build that ladder, we can climb the heights.*[7] This song expressed Mao's sentiments behind his victory proclamation at the Gate of Heavenly Peace. Portraits of both Mao and Stalin as the "benevolent fathers of the state" were posted in town squares, factories, and schools. Mao went to lengths to ensure the Communist indoctrination of every man, woman, and child as millions of copies of his *Quotations from Chairman Mao Zedong* also known as the "little red book" were distributed. He launched a Cultural Revolution Group to silence any opposition from "writers, lecturers and teachers who failed to accept the parties' doctrines" who were either imprisoned, tortured, or executed.[8]

The Emergence of "Pseudo-Capitalist" Reforms in China

Just as Russia lacked any economic advantages under Stalin who devastated the economy until Stalin launched his mass industrialization

---

[6] Robert Service, *Comrades: A History of World Communism* (Cambridge, MA: Harvard University Press, 2007), 283-85.

[7] Service, *Comrades*, 289-90.

[8] Ibid, 334-35.

plans, Mao also weakened the Chinese economy until after his death in 1976 when Deng Xiaoping became successor. Xiaoping was not a rigid adherent to Mao's Little Red Book as he witnessed Western prosperity firsthand when he travelled to France to study and later in Moscow. He knew that the people under Mao's rule were tiring of impoverished conditions with barely enough rice to sustain them. Although Xiaoping was met with opposition from Mao's party loyalists, his ideas for economic reform were soon accepted. Those in the West looked at Xiaoping as a possible ticket for reform. He went on tour of the United States in 1978 and was admirably pictured by the press as he wore a cowboy hat waving and smiling at the crowds. But make no mistake about it – although the West envisioned capitalist reform in China to have them warm up to the ideas of a free republic, Xiaoping remained a hardline Communist party member. Just a year later after his trip to the U.S. he condemned a democracy movement in China by jailing its leaders as a public example and emphasizing his position on Marxist-Lenin policies.[9] Those who did not comply with Xiaoping were either sent to labor camps or executed. The PLA was reorganized as a national defense and security force expanding the military role it had under Mao.

Under Xiaoping, economic reforms for the first time in China's Communist history, private multi-national companies were allowed to set up business in the mainland. Billions of dollars from corporate investors all around the world poured into China's economy with hopes to benefit from this new Asian enterprise. China's gross domestic product increased exponentially. However, what appeared to be outwardly the signs of sincere reform for China was what I call a "pseudo-capitalist" reform. Work conditions for factory workers were unsafe and extremely harsh as workers worked long and grueling hours for meager wages producing tons of cheap products that would flood international markets. Most Chinese company profits did not benefit the workers or their families but went to fund the work of the

---

[9] Service, *Comrades*, 437-39.

CCP. The Chinese people were still under the heavy hand of a totalitarian system. In 1989, students began protesting for democratic and civil rights daily at Tiananmen Square. Many Chinese nationals took notice as pamphlets and literature were circulated calling for government reform. Xiaoping was determined to shut down the protests by declaring martial law. The PLA was sent into the central precincts with orders to clear the protesters. Then to the horror of television viewers around the world a massacre began on June 3, 1989, as tanks rolled across Tiananmen Square and crushed the bodies of protesters under their belted treads. Protest leaders were arrested and sentenced to long terms in labor camps. China may have the appearance of a modern industrial nation, but the appearance is at best a grand deception. It is aptly described by Oxford scholar Robert Service: "Chinese capitalism was red in tooth and claw."[10] After Xiaoping passed in 1997 his successor Xi Jinping assumed leadership of the People's Republic of China and continued to further the international global expansion of the CCP's economic influence. Under Xi the Communist regime continues to this day to suppress any vestige of liberty and freedom in any context – social, religious, or political. Journalists and reporters are censored, and social media and the internet are heavily controlled by the PLA. Millions of Muslims, Buddhists, and Christians alike are imprisoned and tortured. A Chinese Divinity school student that I became good friends with whose name I cannot reveal, told me about his being imprisoned and tortured for a year for his Christian faith, yet he is determined to return to his people to serve the underground church after completing his studies. My friend stated that only the CCP doctrine is permitted to be voiced as the state asserts itself to become the sole religion and philosophy of the people.

---

[10] Service, *Comrades*, 443.

Transforming the International Order Without Firing a Shot

The economic reform that was initiated by Deng Xiaoping in the 1970's is now one of global ambition under Jinping and is one of the most significantly influential political forces impacting every continent on the face of the earth. Jinping's aggressive strategic plan is all within the machinery of the CCP. Professor Clive Hamilton of Sturt University in Australia described this strategic plan this way: "The Chinese Communist Party is determined to transform the international order, to shape the world in its own image without a shot being fired."[11] CCP's strategic plan is certainly attainable given that it has the world's biggest factories financed by foreign investors and leads international product export as the second largest economy. In July 2021, the CCP celebrated their one-hundredth anniversary with 90 million party members and the ability to wield a military force of over 2 million personnel. But CCP's influence cannot be underestimated only in terms of economic or military power but also in its ability to sway global elites, nations, and institutions. The world and mainstream media were shocked when Donald Trump set forth a trade war against China in 2018 for violating the principles of free trade agreement. Beijing is not accustomed to this kind of push-back as most

---

[11] Clive Hamilton and Mareike Ohlberg, *Hidden Hand: How the Chinese Communist Party is Reshaping the World* (London, England: Oneworld Books, 2020), 1.

U.S. Presidents and global leaders have conceded to China's actions without enforcing any international misconduct.

A powerful tool in the CCP's global strategy is known as the "Belt and Road Initiative" (BRI) that funds infrastructure projects worldwide.[12] The BRI is also called the Silk Road and One Belt One Road as a reference to its ancient trading routes with the Europeans back in the time of Marco Polo in the 13th century. The CCP have always presented the BRI as a benevolent program that helps poor nations to develop. However, the BRI is more accurately a tool for reordering the global geo-political system. Jinping has referred to the BRI as a primary component for his vision of building a "community of common destiny for humankind." And in an even bolder admission retired PLA Major-General Qiao Liang declares BRI "as a vehicle to achieve dominance over the U.S. (I will share more later from Liang's PLA warfare manual *Unrestricted Warfare*).

The Tangled CCP Web Within U.S. Government

One way in which the CCP exerts a force of dominance over the U.S. is within our own government. It was in 1970 that the CCP detonated two hydrogen bombs near the Russian border that they sent a message to the world of their position as a military power. Mao invited President Richard Nixon to China to discuss diplomatic relationships between the two superpowers and Henry Kissinger looked at this as an opportunity to offset a power brokerage against Russian. This meeting opened post-cold war relations with the CCP. Ever since then favor has been granted to China through both Democratic and Republican leadership, whereby the CCP has cast a large net of influence through its policies and investments. In 2001, Bill Clinton signed a law passed by Congress that granted permanent trade relations with China which led the way to the CCP benefiting from U.S. investors.[13] Soon after that

---

[12] Hamilton, *Hidden Hand*, 277.

[13] Spalding, *Stealth War*, 30.

China was also accepted as a member of the World Trade Organization. You would think that there would be immediate opposition within the political ranks when a ruthless totalitarian regime is given such esteemed favor. CCP favoritism among American politicians and presidents goes back decades.

I already mentioned the horrific events in Tiananmen Square with the killing of student protestors under Deng Xiaoping, but even more disturbing is a photo of U.S. Security Adviser Brent Scowcroft with Xiaoping that surfaced just a month later smiling at one another with arms outstretched. This was a secret meeting at the direction of President George W. Bush.[14] Bush backed away from criticisms of China's totalitarian rule to welcome free trade agreements with the CCP. His son Neil went on to chair the George H.W. Bush China-U.S. Relations Foundation (CPAFFC) later in 2018. The stated mission of the CPAFFC is to "promote close ties between China and the U.S. and to create a peaceful and prosperous future." In favor of his agency which promotes the building of a "friendly global alliance" Bush spoke quite enthusiastically: "While China is becoming more mature, U.S. democracy is flawed, and politicians are brainwashing Americans into seeing China as a problem."[15] Neil Bush is quite outspoken about the CPAFFC and blames "anti-China" sentiment in the U.S. as a source of tension and that good-will between the two nations must be upheld on the grounds that the U.S. should not meddle in China's affairs. This is the type of rhetoric that Beijing seeks to foster as it creates a stance on non-interference especially as we investigate the origins of the COVID virus.

During Trump's time in office, while most of his administration was taking a harder line on holding the CCP accountable and with Pompeo initiating an investigation into Wuhan for the origins of COVID, there was mounting opposition from both Republicans and Democrats including the mainstream media with accusations of "China-bashing."

---

[14] Robert Spalding, *Stealth War: How China Took Over While America's Elite Slept* (USA: Penguin Random House, 2019), 29.

[15] Hamilton & Ohlberg, *Hidden Hand*, 40-41.

It is interesting that this base had been building for months prior to the pandemic. Now anyone who challenged the bipartisan friendship extended to China is immediately called out for exhibiting a "cold-war" mentality that exudes arrogant nationalism. In March 2019 at a global symposium at Peking University, former Clinton administration deputy assistant secretary of state Susan Shirk made an interesting remark denouncing nationalism and warning of a "McCarthyite Red Scare" looming in the U.S.: "a herding instinct is driving Americans to see China threats everywhere, with potentially disastrous consequences."

Shirk is also joined by many others who favor friendly relations with China. Former State Department official Susan Thornton also is another strong advocate for positive diplomacy with the CCP, believing that it will help encourage China to become a responsible global citizen. In July 2019 just months before the COVID outbreak, Thornton was one of the primary authors of an open international letter drafted and signed by more than a hundred American scholars, foreign policy experts and large corporate executives who rejected Trump's stance against China. While the letter elevates favorable global relations with China, there is no mention of the CCP nor of any potential threat that they pose as a military aggressor or threat to national security. One of the letter's signers is Michael Swaine who is a senior fellow at the Carnegie Endowment for International Peace who condemned America's cold war response and extreme policy stance toward China. Swaine and other members of the Carnegie Endowment portray China as an important leader of the international order seeking to make valuable contributions for global reform.

Just as news of a pandemic in China started to surface, Trump's impeachment trial commenced in the U.S. Senate on January 16, 2020. As early as May 2019, Joe Biden positioned himself among Democratic candidates in Iowa by criticizing the idea that China was a threat to the U.S. In Iowa, he told the audience "China is going to eat our lunch? Come on man! I mean, you know, they're not bad folks. But guess what? They're not competition for us."[16] Of course, Biden has no reason to see China as posing any threat especially when his son Hunter Biden flew to China on Air Force Two with him in December 2013 during his Vice Presidency to make a $1 billion dollar business deal with the Bank of China through an investment fund called Bohai Harvest RST.[17] Joe Biden quipped in Iowa that China was not going to pose competition for the U.S. although it was clearly a means for his son Hunter to profit directly from Communist investments. It is also no secret that Joe Biden has held to a globalist vision that includes China in the forefront of the international order. A foreign policy think-tank whose mission is to advance what it calls a "liberal global agenda" was created on February 8, 2018, in coordination with the University of Pennsylvania and named in honor of Biden: The Penn Biden Center for Diplomacy and Global Engagement.[18] Shortly after Biden assumed office the center was moved to Washington, D.C. It is no surprise that the Penn Biden Center was critical of the Trump administration's hard line on holding China accountable. The center's web site proudly posts an article from the New York Times about Trump's visit to China that can be read in Chinese as well as English which reeks of "anti-American" sentiment praising China's President Xi Jinping for being a powerful global leader and criticizing Trump for being a faltering Nationalist:

The Economist heralded Mr. Xi with an honorific usually reserved for America's president: the world's most powerful man. Mr. Trump stepped off Air Force One in Beijing on Wednesday with historically low job-approval ratings, just hours after suffering a shellacking in off-year elections. His credibility is cratering abroad – polls have shown a drop in confidence

---

[16] Adam Edelman, *Biden's Comments Downplaying China Threat to U.S. Fire Up Pols on Both Sides*, NBC News; May 2, 2019. Accessed November 2, 2021 at https://www.nbcnews.com/politics /2020-election/ biden-s-comments-downplaying-china-threat-u-s-fires-pols-n1001236

[17] Spalding, *Stealth War*, 7.

[18] This site complete with its mission statement can be found at https://global. upenn.edu/penn-biden-center.

in American leadership. As the personal trajectories of Mr. Trump and Mr. Xi diverge, so too does the focus of their leadership. While Mr. Trump is obsessed with building walls, Mr. Xi is busy building bridges.[19]

Interesting – the man who is president of a ruthless totalitarian regime is praised for being a global "bridge builder" and called the world's most powerful leader? This attitude which exalts China and puts down American Nationalism is prevalent not only in the media but also within our own government. The buck coming from China does not only stop with the Biden administration. As mentioned, it runs deep in both Republican and Democrat camps as we have seen. Retired Brigadier General Robert Spalding describes it this way: "I originally suspected that the CCP's conspiracy to infiltrate the United States was an *alliance* between American elites and the CCP. Many of our political leaders regard China as a partner, despite the fact that the CCP has declared itself at war with the West."[20] Spalding goes on to say that ties with our government run deeper than we think when he refers an example with Senate Majority Leader Mitch McConnel who is an outspoken critic of Trump's policies on China. McConnel married Elaine Chao who was George W. Bush's Labor Secretary. Chao's father James Chao is a senior executive of one of China's most prominent global shipping companies and served as the General Secretary in the Chinese Communist Party from 1989 to 2002. It is reported that the Chao family has donated over $1 million dollars to support McConnel's campaigns. And according to McConnel's 2008 Senate Financial Disclosure Report, he and his wife have received gifts from China in value of $25 million. It is apparent that the Communist Chinese government is buying off U.S. politicians as a ticket to ride within the global elite. CCP's collaboration with the "Deep State" sets the backdrop through which we must understand the nature of what happened in Wuhan. Challenges to arriving at the truth

---

[19] Antony J. Blinken, *Trump is Ceding Global Leadership to China*, November 8, 2017. New York Times. Accessed on November 2, 2021 at https://www.nytimes.com/2017 /11/08/opinion/trump-china-xi-jinping.html?_r=0

[20] Spalding, *Stealth War*, 4.

behind the origins of COVID are immense as we consider this deep web of entanglement not only in Wuhan and in our own government but also in the international global order.

Unrestricted Warfare: the PLA Playbook for CCP Global Domination

Not only does the Communist China's web run deep within our nation's political system but they also have powerful influences upon our own military leadership. China is a force to be reckoned with, a powerful military that in addition to conventional warfare is also armed with technologically advanced capabilities that are nuclear, biological, and cyber. Even though many are convinced that China is a benevolent world power seeking the common good for all nations they are still Communist to the core and are committed to an agenda of global domination. They will achieve this through any means possible. A very disturbing trend is the CCP's alliance with some of our high-ranking American military leaders. In late 2020 the Pentagon's Joint Chief of Staff, Mark Milley, contacted General Li Zuocheng of the Communist People's Liberation Army to discuss what he described as concerns that

President Trump's desire to challenge the election results might be seen as a potential threat to China.

Milley tells the PLA General: "General Li, I want to assure you that the American government is stable, and everything is going to be OK. We are not going to attack you or conduct any kinetic operations against you. General Li, you and I have known each other for five years. If we're going to attack, I'm going to call you ahead of time. It's not going to be a surprise."[21] This is shocking and even appears to be treason that a military superior in the Pentagon would be having this conversation with a PLA general about providing the favor of advanced warning for an attack by U.S. Forces. Milley admits that the conversation was carried out without Trump's knowledge. This conversation between Milley and the PLA general Li came to light shortly after the bungled withdrawal of troops from Afghanistan. The pull-out of U.S. Forces now gives China further momentum to expand their Belt and Road Initiative (BRI) in Afghanistan by constructing railroads and gas pipelines throughout Pakistan and Iran. China has been aggressively pursuing the iron ore mining with its $3.5 billion dollar investments into Afghanistan since 2011, as well as the extraction of rare earth minerals in addition to oil and gas development.[22] Not only does the vacuum left by a disastrous U.S. withdrawal create opportunities for economic exploitation, but it clearly provides a military advantage for China falling within their war playbook. Colonel Quiao Liang and Colonel Wang Xiangsui are military strategists whose works have been translated in the document *Un-Restricted Warfare.*

This work was written and published by the PLA Literature and Arts Publishing House in Beijing and represents a more contemporary

---

[21] Tucker Carlson: *Mark Milley Committed Treason, and Others Were Implicated,* Fox News, September 14, 2021. Accessed November 2, 2021 at https://www.foxnews.com/ opinion/tucker-carlson-mark-milley-committed-treason.

[22] Loro Horato, *China's Main Interests in Afghanistan are of a Strategic & Political Nature,* August 10, 2021, Defence Point. Source accessed November 3, 2021 from https://defence-point.com/2021/08/21/china-s-main-interests-in-afghanistan-are-of-a-strategic-and-political-nature/.

strategy for the new generation of CCP soldiers. Its central thesis is stated in the introduction of the translator's note as follows:

Published prior to the bombing of China's embassy in Belgrade, the book has recently drawn the attention of both the Chinese and Western press for its advocacy of a multitude of means, both military and particularly non-military, to strike at the United States during times of conflict. Hacking into websites, targeting financial institutions, using the media, and conducting terrorism and urban warfare are among the methods proposed. In the *Zhongguo Qingnian Bao* interview, Quia was quoted as stating that the **"the first rule of unrestricted warfare is that there are no rules with nothing forbidden."**[23]

The first rule of PLA operations for the defeat of the U.S. and global domination is clearly stated: "there are no rules with nothing forbidden." Those who believe that China will be transparent and forthcoming regarding the origins of COVID, and the Wuhan Lab incident are incredibly gullible. And even worse are those within the Deep State who have been bought out by the deceitfulness of this hostile global power who deny any hypothesis for lab origins and the intent of gain of function research to weaponize COVID. The PLA manual makes some bold assertions about the use of technology in speaking of the "infusion of energy into a technological plague that can be released from Pandora's box." Could this be applied as an application for gain of function research? The PLA manual further adds: "this kind of war means that all means will be in readiness, that information will be omnipresent, and the battlefield will be everywhere." While the term "biowarfare" is not used, there are references to the development of "biotechnology" later mentioned with this statement: "We are by no means denying that, in future warfare, certain advanced weapons may play a leading role." And this is also mentioned in the context of laboratory development:

---

[23] Qiao Liang and Wang Xiangsui, *Un-Restriced Warfare; Translated from the Original People's Liberation Army Documents* (Brattleboro, VT: Echo Point Books & Media, 1999), xvii-xviii.

Building the weapons to fit the fight, an approach which has distinctive features of the age and the characteristics of the laboratory, may not only be viewed as a kind of active choice, it can also be taken as coping with shifting events by sticking to a fundamental principle, and in addition to being a major breakthrough in the history of preparing for war, it also implies the potential crisis in modern warfare: Customizing weapons systems to tactics which are still being explored and studied.[24]

The PLA warfare strategy manual tends to be philosophical in some respects with criticisms of Americans as having a limited concept of a broad application of technology to warfare: "The Americans invariably halt their thinking at the boundary where technology has not reached." It then speaks eloquently of "new biological and chemical weapons" as "new concept weapons whose immediate goal is to kill and destroy."

The PLA "new concept weapons" are described as being different in the sense that they "transcend the domain of traditional weapons, which can be controlled and manipulated at a technical level, which are capable of inflicting material or psychological casualties on an enemy." We are told that these new concept weapons will be nothing short of astonishing: "The new concept weapons will cause ordinary people and military men alike to be greatly astonished at the fact that commonplace things that are close to them can also become weapons with which to engage war." Could this reference to the new concept weapons include common place things like viral pathogens that can be weaponized? The PLA manual continues further to explain the benefit of this in the context of "kinder weapons:"

What is the point of defeating the enemy if it means risking the destruction of the world? How do we avoid warfare that results in ruin for all? A "balance of terror" involving "mutually assured destruction" was the immediate product of this thinking, but its by-product was to

---

[24] Liang & Xingsui, *Un-Restricted Warfare*, 16-20.

provide a braking mechanism for the runaway express of improving the lethal capabilities of weapons.[25]

The "kinder weapons" tactic is a reference to the strategic sensibility of killing your enemy without obliterating his property, cities, and land as in the case of a nuclear attack. If your enemy is dead and his land is intact, then it provides a strategic advantage for occupation. We will discuss later that this is the advantage gained by the deployment of chemical or biological weapons so the conqueror can occupy the lands of his enemy and not destroy it. The PLA does confirm this strategic advantage with the deployment of these kinder new concept weapons:

The trend to "kinder" weapons is nothing other than a reflection in the production and development of weapons of this great change in man's cultural background. At the same time, technological progress has given us the means to strike at the enemy's nerve center directly without harming other things, giving us numerous new options for achieving victory, and all these make people believe that the best way to achieve victory is to control, not to kill.[26]

The PLA manual then adds the superiority of technology for the development of these weapons: "Today we have enough technology, and we can create many methods of causing fear which are more effective." So here are the two primary axioms straight out of the CCP war manual: "control and fear." Unleashing a viral pandemic certainly will achieve the opportunity for control and fear in the global order.

The PLA manual refers to an expansion of Mao's CCP principle "every citizen a soldier" with a new technologically elite military developing modern weapons that "can attack the enemy from a place beyond his range." The new warfare arena referred to as "Military Operations Other Than War" (MOOTW). This includes various sectors such as trade, information, and finance—where George Soros is

---

[25] Ibid, 17-18.

[26] Liang & Xingsui, *Un-Restricted Warfare*, 18.

mentioned as an example of global influence in financial institutions and CNN is mentioned as an example of global influence and media. CNN is hailed as the paragon of message control according to the PLA. These are praised as the MOOTW weapons that can be directed at China's enemies. For China, the new concept weapons go beyond conventional warfare with the application of technology to deploy bio-technology as a means of world conquest. We now turn our attention to the rudimentary components of biological warfare.

Chapter 2

An Introduction to Bioweapons 101

Acts of terrorism, including bioterrorism, generate fear and panic through their utterly unpredictable nature; the next attack could happen anywhere at any time with any number of weapons. – Anthony S. Fauci's forward to the Journal of the American Medical Association's (JAMA) Bioterrorism: *Guidelines for Medical and Public Health Management*

A ccording to the Weapons of Mass Destruction (WMD) Statute, Title 18 U.S.C. Section 2332a bioterrorism is defined as "the threat (or conspiracy) to use a weapon of mass destruction, including any biological agent, toxin, or vector against a national of the United States or within the United States."[27] The *Criminal & Epidemiological Handbook* which was a manual that I used in my career training later adds "The term WMD includes any weapons involving a disease organism. However, it does not require the biological agent be a 'select agent' only that the agent is capable of causing biological malfunction, disease or death in a living organism" and cites Title 18 U.S.C. Section 178 in the National Select Agent Registry. What is meant by "select agents" is explained in the manual's footnote meaning that a

---

[27] *Criminal & Epidemiological Investigation Handbook*; 2011 edition: U.S. Department of Justice Federal Bureau of Investigation, page 11.

biological weapon does not have to be limited to the registry's list of conventional bioweapons that are in the standard category A and B agents (we will discuss more on these agents later). A basic definition comes from the U.S. Armed Forces Manual: "Biological attack is the intentional use, by an enemy of live agents or toxins to cause death and disease among citizens, animals, and plants."[28] More specifically the broader application of biological weapons that can be used by terrorist groups, as well as enemies foreign or domestic and can essentially include a weaponized disease organism or viral pathogen. Dr. Victor W. Sidel a professor at Montefiore Medical Center and the Albert Einstein College of Medicine, who has written with particular emphasis on China and provided consultation for the World Health Organization (WHO), mentions that of all forms of conventional weapons, biological weapons "may inspire the most fear – because they are not visible, they are easy to disseminate, can spread easily from person to person, and can cause horrific diseases."[29] Sidel also addresses the proliferation of biological weapons by providing us with this definition: "Biological weapons are living organisms – usually microorganisms – or their toxic products used intentionally to cause illnesses or death in humans, animals, or plants. They are produced or used with the goal of causing illness or death in humans, limiting food supplies or agricultural resources, and evoking fear in populations."[30]

Papers submitted for publication in the Journal of the American Medical Association (JAMA) tell the research of the Working Group on Civilian Biodefense comprised of subject matter experts from academia and government defense in 1998 set forth to identify the pathogens

---

[28] Dick Couch, *The U.S. Armed Forces Nuclear, Biological, & Chemical Survival Manual: Everything You Need to Know to Protect Yourself & Your Family From the Growing Terrorist Threat*, (New York, NY: Perseus Books, 2003), 58.

[29] Barry S. Levy and Victor W. Sidel, *Terrorism & Public Health: A Balanced Approach to Strengthening Systems and Protecting People* (New York, NY: Oxford University Press, 2003), 175.

[30] Ibid, 176.

that have the potential to be used as bioweapons against civilian populations.[31] The workgroup stated that the most dangerous bioweapons are those able to impact populations with high morbidity or mortality rates, high transmissibility from person to person, having novel viral characteristics for which there is initially limited effective treatment, and wide-scale viral replication properties. Rarely a single agent can fit all these criteria, while a possible combination of biological agents may have this ability especially if they have been synthetically enhanced or in the case of the Title 18 code in section 178 mentioned previously to include a description of agents that are capable of "biological malfunction." It is interesting to note that the SARS-CoV-2 does easily fit all the categories for dangerous pathogens that can be weaponized – high morbidity and mortality, high transmissibility from person to person and for having novel characteristics causing challenges in limited treatment. We will address this further in relation to gain of function (GOF) research.

Overview of Biological Agents

We will first address biological agent categories briefly before moving into a historical overview. There are three categories by which biological agents are classified: Category A – high priority agents that pose a risk to national security because they can be easily disseminated or transmitted from person to person that can cause high mortality and high morbidity, Category B – agents that are moderately easy to disseminate causing moderate morbidity and low mortality, and Category C – agents that could be engineered for mass dissemination with the potential for high morbidity and high mortality causing major health impact.[32]

---

[31] Tara O'Toole, Thomas V. Inglesby, and Donald A. Henderson, *Why Understanding Biological Weapons Matters to Medical & Public Health Professionals* compiled within *Bioterrorism: guidelines for Medical & Public Health Management* (The American Medical Association, 2002), 1.

[32] Levy and Sidel, *Terrorism & Public Health*, 182-83.

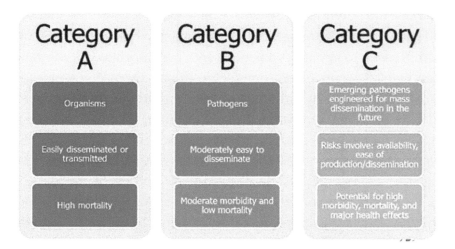

Let's start with Category A agents that include high profile disease causing viral pathogens such as anthrax (*Bacillus anthracis*), plague (*Yersinia pestis*), smallpox (*Variola major*) and Viral hemorrhagic fevers such as Ebola. After the 911 attacks, these agents raised the greatest concern because of intelligence reports which claimed the intent of terrorist cells to weaponize these against the U.S. At the time, the George W. Bush administration also suspected Iraq of having weapons of mass destruction (WMD's). Part of this suspicion was based on previous attacks that Saddam Hussein used chemical weapons against Kurdish guerillas in the late 1980's. Although there was never any solid confirmation that Iraq possessed WMD's after the Gulf War, U.S. the Bush administration appropriated considerable resources for biodefense and emergency preparedness capabilities through Homeland Security Presidential Directive 21 (HSPD-21). HSPD-21 "established a National Security Strategy for Public Health and Medical Preparedness set forth in *Biodefense for the 21st century* (April 2004)."[33] This directive that partly funded the work at my department stated the mission "would transform our national

---

[33] Homeland Security Presidential Directive (HSPD-21), George W. Bush authorized for press release on October 18, 2007. Source Acquired November 4, 2021 from https://irp.fas.org/ offdocs/nspd/hspd-21.htm.

approach to protecting the health of the American people" by establishing programs for bio surveillance, epidemiologic surveillance, and bioterrorism emergency preparedness.

The only Category A incident occurred when powdered anthrax was mailed shortly after 911 that claimed the lives of five individuals. There were no terrorist cells behind the incident, the lead suspect believed to be a rogue scientist at the bioweapons lab at Fort Detrick committed suicide just before FBI agents apprehended him.[34] The early bioterrorism program where I was assigned in North Texas (we called it B/T) also developed medical countermeasures for smallpox attacks and started vaccinating critical response teams for the virus. This was soon discontinued because the risks of deploying vaccine with smallpox virus outweighed the benefits. Another time when there was a Category A agent concern, I was assigned to Logistics Incident Command in North Texas to work with the emergency response teams after an Ebola source case in 2014 died and infected two nurses. Since Ebola is classified as a Category A agent, we had to be briefed by the Dallas FBI WMD Unit Director as their surveillance teams picked up on some chatter that terrorist cells indicated interest in stealing medical waste contaminated with Ebola to weaponize it. Within a year of the U.S. Ebola exposures the virus was contained until July 2019 just a few months before the COVID outbreak in Wuhan we started receiving early reports of Ebola cases surging in the Democratic Republic of Congo. For nearly six months prior I had directed my planning unit to begin updating our pandemic response plans and got approval to proceed with putting together our subject matter expert team for the project. When Ebola came on the radar that summer of 2019, I was told by my superiors to drop our pandemic response planning project and focus our resources on monitoring the Ebola outbreak, as well, and to conduct mass training exercises for Ebola response and containment. Although I did not perceive Ebola to be an imminent threat in the U.S. and I felt that there was a greater

---

[34] Anthrax Investigation "Amerithrax" Federal Bureau of Investigation, https://www.fbi.gov/history /famous-cases/amerithrax-or-anthrax-investigation.

need to focus our efforts upon pandemic response capabilities, I reluctantly complied. Then when COVID started ramping up in early 2020, elected officials inquired why our unit had not updated our pandemic response plans. My reply to them simply was that "I followed orders to discontinue our pandemic planning project to focus on Ebola," and I sent records of emails to substantiate that, as well. During my years with the B/T preparedness program we spent hundreds of hours conducting training exercises and response plans for Category A agents, but (thankfully) there was never a biological attack carried out on American soil with this agent. However, our resources would have been better utilized in preparation for Category C agent response planning which was addressed only at a minimal level.

Category B agents includes pathogens such as Brucellosis (*Brucella*), Glanders (*Burkhoderia*), Ricin (*Ricinus*), and Encephalitis. These agents pose a much lower risk for moderate morbidity and mortality, and therefore, only require standard local health department surveillance protocols. However, the Category C Agents have the greater potential for systematic classification in the context of SARS-CoV-2 considering gain of GOF research. If my hypothesis is correct that SARS-CoV-2 originated in a lab through GOF research by direct manipulation of DNA/RNA genetic viral constructs then the Category C classification can be met as given—***emerging pathogens that could be engineered*** *for mass dissemination in the future because of availability, ease of production and dissemination, and potential for high morbidity and mortality and major health impact.* If the COVID virus was manipulated through genetic engineering whether it was leaked from a lab accidentally or was released intentionally, Category C will apply in this first instance. A second instance of Category C classification would be related to its specific viral listing as a "Nipah" virus (*Nipa henipavirus*). The bat-borne Nipah virus genome which has a Category C classification is a single-stranded RNA composed of six structural proteins and is commonly associated with outbreaks in South and Southeast Asia. Structural proteins are an important component for viral cross-sequencing in GOF research and make Nipah virus a compatible candidate for pairing with SARS-CoV-2 spiked protein clusters. Dr. Steven Quay who has done extensive research on SARS-CoV-2 origins submitted a study with several other scientists regarding virus samples from the Wuhan Lab that were contaminated with the Nipah virus. Quay stated that some of the viral sequences were found in infectious cloning vectors of the type used for genetic manipulation.[35] The data sets were originally sequenced in a study by one of the chief zoonotic researchers who specializes in the analysis of viral specimens from bats at the Wuhan Lab, Dr. Shi Zhengli. If there was a deliberate attempt at genetic engineering of SARS-CoV-2 with other viral genomes, then we may have the support to substantiate a bioweapons hypothesis for COVID-19 especially as a weaponized Category C agent of mass destruction. More on this later when we discuss the "stealth design" of the virus in Chapter 4.

A Brief History of Modern Biological Warfare

---

[35] Steven C. Quay, Monali Rahalkar, Adrian Jones and Rahul Bhulikar, *Contamination or Vaccine Research? RNA Sequencing data of early COVID-19 patient samples show abnormal presence of vectorized H7N9 hemagglutinin segment.* Abstract published July 3, 2021. Source document available at https://zenodo.org/ record/5067706#.YYQ-TkrMKUl.

In World War I, Germany utilized glanders, mustard gas, and anthrax against European troops. This prompted the first convention calling for the "prohibition of biological weapons" in Geneva on June 17, 1925, but the signing of this declaration would only be short-lived. In the 1930's, Japan dropped glass bomblets from military aircraft that broke open upon impact in villages in mainland China that spread plague *(Yersinia pestis)*.[36] Then later In World War II, the Nazis tested biological weapons on concentration camp prisoners. After these two world wars, there was a concentrated effort by industrialized western nations for the research and development of biological weapons. Superpowers who were involved with the race to add bioweapons to their arsenal included the United States, Great Britain, Russia, and China. In the United States, the U.S. Army Medical Research Institute of Infectious Diseases (USAMRIID) was established at Fort Detrick, Maryland. Later calls for greater international reform were called by the United Nations Committee on Disarmament to limit the stockpiling of all WMD's in 1975 to include both nuclear and biological weapons.[37] Although there was a recognized membership of 183 "States Parties and Four Signatory States" that responded, other than the U.S. and NATO nations who took some steps toward arms reduction, Russia and China did not provide any solid confirmation of follow through with the reduction of biological weapons. In the middle East, Iran, Iraq, Syria, Turkey, Egypt, Sudan, Saudi Arabia, and Israel are said to either possess biological weapons or access to the technology to produce them.

Even after the Biological Weapons Convention, the Soviet Union and Communist China continued to produce and stockpile biological weapons. Russia had the most aggressive weapons program with over 42,000 scientists who were also developing weapons delivery systems

---

[36] Levy and Sidel, *Terrorism & Public Health*, 177-80.

[37] United Nations Office for Disarmament Affairs, https://www.un.org/disarmament/biological-weapons.

for deploying biological agents to their enemy targets.[38] China follows Russia in its production of biological weapons. According to an August 2019 U.S. State Department report

The People's Republic of China has possessed an offensive biological warfare program from the early 1950'. China continues to develop its biotechnology infrastructure and available information on studies from researchers at Chinese military medical institutions that identify biological activities of a possibly anomalous nature since presentations discuss identifying, characterizing, and testing numerous toxins with potential dual-use applications.[39]

Bioengineering of Viral Pathogens

According to the U.S. Army Medical Research Institute of Infectious Diseases' (USMRIID) *Medical Management of Biological Casualties Handbook* "viruses are the simplest microorganisms and consist of a nucleocapsid protein coat containing genetic material, either RNA or DNA." This makes them ideal for virus-specific host cells to be cultivated in synthetic nutrient solutions and then infected with other viruses and enhanced through further manipulation at a genetic level in a laboratory environment. This new era of technological advancement in bioengineering in GOF research not only provides benefits for medical applications, but it also is a two-edged sword which contributes to the creation of bioweapons of mass destruction, as well. USMRIID provides further details bioengineered weapons can have significant global impact:

Once a new disease is introduced into a suitable human population, it often spreads rapidly and with devastating impact on the medical and public health infrastructure. If the disease is severe, it may

---

[38] Levy and Sidel, *Terrorism & Public Health*, 179.

[39] *Adherence to and Compliance with Arms Control, Nonproliferation, and Disarmament Agreements & Comments*, published and prepared by the U.S. Department of State, Section 5.1, page 45.

lead to social disruption, and cause severe economic impact. Emerging disease outbreaks may be difficult to distinguish from the intentional introduction of infectious diseases for nefarious purposes; consideration must be given to this possibility before any novel infectious disease outbreak is deemed to be of a natural origin.[40]

This section from USMRIID's handbook titled *Emerging Threats and Future Biological Weapons* provides us with interesting implications for our SARS-CoV-2 bioweapons hypothesis. First, such a weapon could have considerable and far-reaching adverse impacts to cause social disruption and economic loss. Secondly, a bioengineered weapon "may be difficult to distinguish" from a naturally occurring pandemic. Therefore, the advice is given directly from USMRIID to first consider the possibility that an outbreak could be the result of a bioweapon rather than natural origin. We will discuss in Chapter Four why the propaganda narrative strongly denied a biological weapons or laboratory hypothesis for SARS-CoV-2 despite USMRIID's directive. The mainstream media pushed an exclusive natural origin theory, condemning a lab or bioweapons hypothesis as "anti-science." The USMRIID's handbook which was one of my field guides and reference manuals in my bioterrorism preparedness career offers sage wisdom for how we should have approached SARS-CoV-2 outbreak and pandemic:

As scientists develop more sophisticated laboratory procedures and increase their understanding of molecular biology and the human genetic code, the possibility of bioengineering more virulent, antibiotic-resistant, and vaccine-resistant pathogens for nefarious uses becomes increasingly likely. It is already theoretically possible to synthesize and weaponize certain biological response modifiers (BMRs) as well as to engineer genomic weapons capable of inserting novel DNA into host cells.[41]

---

[40] *USAMRIID's Medical Management of Biological Casualties Handbook*, 6th edition, April 2005. (Frederick MD – Ft. Detrick, 2005), 117, 204-205.

[41] *USAMRIID's Medical Management of Biological Casualties Handbook*, 205.

This is also timely for our lab hypothesis considering that SARS-CoV-2 is a novel virus for which there is little natural immunity or protection in its initial spread. Furthermore, this concept of bioengineered modification at the genetic level was especially developed in the Soviet Union and Communist China.

Ken Alibek was a chief research and development scientist for Soviet Union bioweapons who defected to the U.S. Alibek tells of a highly classified Soviet program that was launched by Communist Party General Secretary Lenoid Brezhnev named the "Enzyme Project," which was dedicated to the bioengineering of viral pathogens for weapons of mass destruction. The research and development project "aimed to modernize existing biological weapons and to develop genetically altered pathogens, resistant to antibiotics and vaccines, which could be turned into powerful weapons for use in intercontinental warfare."[42] The nation's best biologists, epidemiologists and biochemists were recruited into the project along with Alibek. Project Enzyme's covert bioengineering military research and development installations operated under the disguise of pharmaceutical or medical research institutions. The Soviet Academy of Sciences maintained the project into four distinct institutions: Institute of Protein, Institute of Molecular Biology, Institute of Biochemistry, and the Institute of Bioorganic Chemistry. Between 1979 to 1989, the Soviet Union conducted large-scale tests of biological agent deployment simulations with aerosolization from aircraft (spraying biological agents over highly populated areas) and ballistic missiles with bioweapon payloads. According to Alibek in the late 1980's, more than sixty thousand personnel were dedicated to Project Enzyme. Mikhail Gorbachev later authorized over $200 million for the project in the 1990's.

---

[42] Ken Alibek with Stephen Handelman, *Biohazard: The Chilling True Story of the Largest Covert Biological Weapons Program in the World — Told from the Inside by the Man Who Ran It* (New York, NY: Dell Publishing, 1999), 41.

Communist China also comes to the forefront of bioengineering pathogens into weapons. In a report that China submitted to the 2011 United Nations Bioweapons Convention titled "Creation of Man-Made Pathogens," they acknowledged the potential of this research for "targeted delivery technology."[43] In an internal State Department report, Mike Pompeo and Miles Yu addressed China's bioweapons capabilities: "China has been conducting research on dangerous dual-use biological and genetic technologies that are prone to causing global pandemics."[44] This was documented by Australian investigative journalist Sharri Markson and her research team who have done phenomenal work detailing the biowarfare projects of the CCP and PLA in their book: *What Really Happened in Wuhan: A Virus Like No Other, Countless Infections, Millions of Deaths*. Markson further adds that the dual use of GOF research by China could be a violation of the Biological Weapons Convention (BWC) according to Tom DiNanno the Assistant Secretary of the Arms Control, Verification and Compliance Bureau. The U.S. State Department obtained a 2015 research document from the PLA titled *The Unnatural Origin of SARS and New Species of Man-Made Viruses as Genetic Bioweapons* which describes how SARS coronaviruses could be deployed as genetically designed bioweapons.[45] If this document is authentic, it does show a link between Chinese military GOF research and the SARS virus, which also has implications for the origin of SARS-CoV-2. We will look at ties between the Chinese military (PLA) and Wuhan Institute of Virology in the next chapter.

---

[43] Bill Gertz, *China Deception Fuels Fear of Biological Weapons Ethnic Experiments*, The Washington Times, May 14, 2020. Source acquired November 8, 2021 at https://www.washingtontimes.com/news/2020/ may/14/ china-deception-fuels-fears-biological-weapons-eth/.

[44] Sharri Markson, *What Really Happened in Wuhan: A Virus Like No Other; Countless Infections, Millions of Deaths*, (New York, NY: Harper Collins, 2021), 306.

[45] Stephen Chen, *The Chinese Book at the Bottom of the SARS Bioweapons Claims*, South China Morning Post, October 5, 2021. Source accessed on November 9, 2021, from https://www.msn.com/en-xl/news/other/ the-chinese-book-at-the-bottom-of-the-sars-bioweapons-claims/ar-BB1gzDAb

Delivery & Deployment of Biological Agents

Methods for the delivery of a biological agent are not without challenges. Biological warfare has considerable research into the deployment of agents that are more specifically referred to as "munitions" or the devices and mechanisms to release a biological pathogen into a local population.[46] "Point-source" delivery systems may include the use of bomblets (glass vials) that when dropped from aircraft break open releasing biological agents. Such munition systems that involve aerosolization or the spraying of biological agent in a fine mist are also referred to as "line-source" delivery. However, this means can have severe limitations due to the unpredictable factors in meteorological conditions such as wind, humidity and temperature that can prevent an aerosolized delivery from being effective. I recall a mass bioterrorism response training exercise that I was part of in North Texas that included the use of an agricultural crop duster to release anthrax spores (*bacillus anthracis*) over a sports stadium crowded with spectators. However, we soon learned after our consultation with a meteorologist that something as simple as the wind and temperature could seriously impede the effectiveness of such an attack scenario. Simple elements of biology prevent the use of explosive devices or conventional bombs as intense heat easily kills off living organisms. This is the challenge of using ballistic missile payloads. According to former Soviet bioweapons scientist Ken Alibek, in addition to delivery challenges there are considerable challenges in stockpiling unstable agents for extended periods of time.[47]

---

[46] *Jane's CBRN Response Handbook,* 4th edition, 195-197.

[47] Albek, *Biohazard,* 98-99.

Given serious limitations to bioweapon munitions and their stock-piling or storage, how can an enemy most effectively deploy biological pathogens over a large population? C.J. Peters, an epidemiologist who has extensive experience as a commander in U.S. military virology and has been in the forefront of mitigation and response in the nation's Ebola outbreak, addresses the attempts to weaponize natural diseases. Peters states that the most lethal delivery system for biological agents is the most natural: "The most formidable kind of biological agent is one that spreads from animal to animal or person to person."[48] A virus is an efficient killing machine that is designed to replicate in an animal or human host that can carry it to infect others. The mass dissemina-tion of a virus is more effectively transmitted through "human muni-tion systems." No stockpiling or storage is required, once a human host is infected, then they become the means to deployment of the bio-logical pathogen. If the viral pathogen can be genetically enhanced to have a greater transmission and infection rate, it will spread quickly on a global scale. U.S. Airforce Colonel Michael J. Ainscough presented a counterproliferation paper in 2002 to the Air War College titled *Next Generation of Bioweapons,* describing the deployment and impact of bioengineered weapons:

---

[48] C.J. Peters and Mark Olshaker, *Virus Hunter: Thirty Years of Battling Hot Viruses Around the World* (New York, NY: Random House Anchor Books, 1997), 282.

A terrorist attack with a biologically engineered agent may unfold unlike any previous event. The pathogen may be released clandestinely so there will be a delay between exposure and onset of symptoms. Days to weeks later, when people do develop symptoms, they could immediately start spreading contagious diseases. By that time, many people will likely be hundreds of miles away from where they were originally exposed, possibly at multiple international sites. Acutely ill victims may present themselves in large numbers to emergency rooms and other medical treatment facilities. In this scenario, medical professionals would be "on the front lines" of the attack. If the pathogen was highly contagious, medics would then become secondarily infected. Unsuspecting hospitals would become contaminated and soon overwhelmed. This would necessitate the quarantine of a large number of people, with the situation exacerbated by the declining numbers of medical care givers. The media would contribute to public anxiety. Civil disorder and chaos may ensue. We have very little experience in coping with such an epidemic. Advanced warning of an impending specific bioterrorist incident, especially with a genetically engineered BW agent, will be extremely rare – similar to an emerging disease outbreak. Unless we happen to have excellent intelligence, we can only be prepared to respond after the fact.[49]

Col. Ainscough's scenario plays out with a sense of *de'ja' vu* as we recall events that occurred in 2020 at the height of a global pandemic; infected persons hundreds of miles away from the virus source overwhelmed hospitals and medical staff, media created panic, civil disorder and chaos. His paper warned of the impact of such a bioengineered weapon. To create such precise biological engineering would require a laboratory environment capable of research and development and even more specifically GOF specialization. We now will look at the Wuhan Institute of Virology as a possible environment for our SARS-CoV-2 bioweapons hypothesis.

---

[49] Michael J. Ainscough, Col., USAF, *Next Generation Bioweapons: The Technology of Genetic Engineering Applied to Biowarfare & Bioterrorism.* The Counterproliferation Papers Future Warfare Series No. 14. USAF Counterproliferation Center, Maxwell AFB, Alabama, 26.

CHAPTER 3

COVID-19 GROUND ZERO: THE WUHAN INSTITUTE OF VIROLOGY

The Wuhan Institute of Virology's links to the military raise broader concerns about Western science funding China's military modernization. Effectively, France, the UK, the US and other countries are funding research that could be used for nefarious purposes. – Sharri Markson, *What Really Happened in Wuhan*

The city of Wuhan is the capital of the Hubei Province in the People's Republic of China and with over eleven million inhabitants is considered as one of the most populous cities located in central China. On a comparative scale, Wuhan is five times greater than the size of Houston, Texas with a population more than the cities of New York and Chicago combined. Wuhan is not only considered as a manufacturing hub, but it also is a leader in technological sciences that is home to automobile manufacturers, two prestigious universities, 350 research institutes and 1,656 high tech enterprises. The city ranks thirteenth internationally as a leader in scientific research. Wuhan is quite prosperous economically, as it was reported to have a Gross Domestic Product (GDP) of $224 billion in 2018.

The Wuhan Institute of Virology (WIV) lab remains the crown jewel of scientific research at the forefront of China's technological revolution. Located in the hills just outside of the city, it functions as a high-security level four biosafety lab facility. Level four biosafety or BSL-4 labs have the highest safety and security designation as they are specifically designed to conduct research for dangerous pathogens which are highly contagious and have no known medical cure. The official WIV Chinese website details its history back to the Wuhan Institute of Microbiology built in 1956 under the Chinese Academy of Sciences.[50] The current lab was constructed as a partnership with the Jean Merieux BSL-4 Lab in Lyon, France, who intended that there would be an insured cooperation with research projects, but China did not fulfill its part honoring this partnership agreement.[51] It took ten years to construct the lab with the assistance of French subject matter experts with the purpose of providing consultation to the Chinese for lab safety and assistance with future accreditation. Soon after the lab's accreditation in 2018, French

---

[50] Wuhan Institute of Virology (cas.cn), accessed June 28, 2021, from http://english.whiov.cas.cn/.

[51] Eleanor Bartow, *France Warned US in 2015 About China's Wuhan Lab, Investigator Says*, The Daily Signal, July 18, 2021. Source obtained November 9, 2021 from https://www.dailysignal.com/2021/07/28/france-warned-us-in-2015-about-chinas-wuhan-lab-investigator-says/.

scientists were no longer granted continued access in Wuhan. According to a House Foreign Affairs Committee Investigative Report released in August 2021 the Wuhan Lab requested from France biotech equipment of a sensitive nature during their early construction phases. The nature of this request raised concerns within French intelligence: "The PRC was suspected of having a biological warfare program, and the military and intelligence services were worried that the dual-use technology required to build a BSL-4 lab could be misused by the PRC government."[52] The report further adds that the French government rejected the equipment request from the WIV on the grounds of the suspicions held by their ministry of defense that the People's Republic of China (PRC) was seeking to engage in military research. The WIV is home to one of the world's largest virus banks that has catalogued more than 1500 viral strains and has a 32,000 square foot research lab.[53] A report from the Georgian U.S. Embassy in Tbilsi also discloses that the WIV has collaborated on publications and secret projects with China's military on publications and secret projects and since 2017, has engaged in classified research on its behalf.[54]

According to a CDC report the WIV received accreditation as a biosafety level 4 lab (BSL-4) which can handle the most lethal viral pathogens that have limited means of medical countermeasures.[55] The official

---

[52] *The Origins of COVID-19: An Investigation of the Wuhan Institute of Virology.* August 2021. House Foreign Affairs Committee Report Minority Staff, Michael T. McCaul; One Hundred Seventeenth Congress.

[53] *China's Wuhan Institute of Virology, the Lab at the Core of the Coronavirus Controversy*, source obtained November 9, 2021, from https://www.livemint.com/news/world/world/china-s-wuhan-institute-of-virology-the-lab-at-the-core-of-a-virus-controversy-11587266870143.html

[54] U.S. Embassy Tbilisi in Georgia. Site accessed June 21, 2021 at https://ge.usembassy.gov/ fact-sheet-activity-at-the-wuhan-institute-of-virology/

[55] Han Xia, Yi Huang, Haixia Ma, Bobo Liu, Weiwei Xie, Donglin Song, & Zhiming Yuan, Emerging Infectious Diseases Online Report; Vol. 25, No. 5. May 2019. *Biosafety Level 4 Laboratory User Training Program, China* Centers for Disease Control & Prevention. Accessed November 9, 2021 from https://wwwnc.cdc.gov/eid/article/25/5/18-0220_article

Chinese website for the WIV they make the claim: "Pathogenic study of emerging infectious diseases has become one of the major research fields. Great achievements have been made in animal origin studies of Severe Acute Respiratory Syndrome coronavirus (SARS-CoV-2) and avian influenza viruses." Consistent with its focus of research in "animal origin studies", WIV continues to stand by its claims that SARS-CoV-2 had exclusively natural origins. The natural origin theory of SARS-CoV-2 promoted by the Chinese government and most of the global scientific community along with mainstream media has remained their preferred narrative since the beginning of the pandemic.

The Influence of the Wuhan Lab in the West

In the first chapter we talked about the ambitions of the CCP for asserting itself as powerful force for global dominance. To strategically advance its Communist agenda, China is a mastermind in its exploitation of international partnerships. Through these partnerships the CCP secretly gains access to technology, research, and development, health and medical institutions, universities, and the intellectual elites who influence international policy and decision making. Understanding this global ambition of the CCP also is an important consideration for realizing how the WIV of Wuhan has gained access to key strategic partnerships in its global alliance. This assertive dominance of both the CCP and the PLA have been instrumental in positioning the WIV research lab in Wuhan to be a recipient of Western funding and technology from several governments and institutions. There are three primary areas of influence that the CCP uses to elevate the Wuhan Virology Research Lab to this level: (1) Personnel Exchange – the trading of scientists, researchers, and university academics (2) Science and Technology Partnerships – the collaboration of technological research programs, and (3) Western University Partnerships – the collaboration of the academic community and institutions.

The first area of strategic positioning in the exchange of critical infrastructure personnel is carried out through the CCP's organization known as the China Association for International Exchange of Personnel (CAIEP) which maintains a low profile.[56] This association is managed by the Chinese State Administration of Foreign Expert Affairs and reports directly to the Chinese Ministry of Science and Technology which is also linked to the Wuhan Lab. The CAIEP has offices in the U.S., Canada, Russia, Germany, the UK, Australia, Israel, Japan, Singapore, and Hong Kong. Its mission is the aggressive exchange of key personnel from China to work in major industrial firms. However, the CAIEP has gained access to industrial and military technology. In 1999, there was an incident involving China stealing classified nuclear technology through CAIEP contacts with American scientists and engineers. In 2019, CAIEP personnel were arrested in their New York office when it was discovered that they were recruiting American scientists, engineers, and information technology specialists to steal intellectual property for the CCP. Another incident unfolded with the CAIEP attempting to recruit U.S. engineers in the military stealth missile program to obtain highly classified research.

The second area of influence in the U.S. that the CCP and PLA has is through the Chinese Association for Science and Technology USA (CAST-USA). The WIV and PLA military research have access to American military, industrial, and medical technology through this association of more than 10,000 members that include scientists and engineers. The CAST-USA serves as a bridge between the U.S. and China for scientific and technological collaboration. This agency has considerable influence in Washington as there are over 1000 members drawn from Maryland, Virginia, and D.C. In 2002, the University of Maryland partnered with CAST-USA to host a conference for "Chinese Innovation." Another area of influence for the Chinese CAST-USA is in the Silicon Valley, which has nearly one in ten high tech employees

---

[56] Hamilton & Ohlberg, *Hidden Hand*, 152-155.

who have dual citizenship in the U.S. and China. The organization known as the Silicon Valley Chinese Engineers Association was created in 1989 for mainland Chinese experts living in the Bay Area and promoted favorably by California's state government. The stated mission of the Chinese Silicon Valley organization is "establish channels to allow members to engage in China's rapid economic development." These CCP organizations are in good favor with both Democrat and Republican politicians who benefit from generous gifts from the Chinese. In the first chapter, we mentioned Senate Majority Leader Mitch McConnel who received more than $25 million in gifts from China. When the Trump administration in 2019 began to closely scrutinize the America's scientific and technological associations with China, there was a firestorm of criticism that Trump was resorting to a "new McCarthyism."

The third area of influence that the CCP and PLA has is within our own American Universities. Clive Hamilton describes this relationship with academia as follows:

Western universities have been the target of intensive influence efforts by the CCP for some years. Their scientists have been invited to collaborate with Chinese universities, including the PLA's National Laboratory of Defense Technology, and Western universities have also invited Chinese scientists and engineers into their labs, to work on military related research projects. As a result, universities in the West have been helping China to gain military superiority over the U.S. through advanced weapons research.[57]

Under the administration of Hu-Wen in Beijing, Chinese Communists developed the Confucius Institutes. Although the Confucius Institutes stated that its mission was to promote teaching of the Chinese language and culture in foreign universities, it was more along the lines of CCP propaganda. By July 2019, there were a total of ninety American universities that provided an office for the

---

[57] Hamilton & Ohlberg, *Hidden Hand*, 155.

Confucius Institutes. Along with the Confucius Institutes another significant collaborative Chinese program working with foreign universities is the "Thousand Talents Program" which recruits highly qualified ethnic Chinese people to return to China with their subject matter expertise in science, technology, and military fields of knowledge. The Chinese students enroll in American Universities to obtain PhD's in various fields and some even act as "sleeper agents." What is most disturbing is China's Thousand Talents program's ties to the WIV and the American National Institutes of Health.

The National Institutes of Health Ties to Wuhan

The National Institutes of Health (NIH) located in Bethesda, Maryland is the nation's largest biomedical research agency that is part of the U.S. Department of Health and Human Services (USHHS) and the Centers for Disease Control and Prevention (CDC). The NIH has established itself in several fields including public health epidemiology and disease virology. In 2019, there were concerns being raised regarding the theft of intellectual property from various American universities by the Chinese. MD Anderson is a cancer research hospital in Houston, Texas that is partly funded by the NIH. An incident occurred at MD Anderson with the firing of three Chinese American researchers over suspicion of research theft. All three researchers had been part of the Thousand Talents program.[58] A senior faculty member, Dr. Charles Lieber at Harvard University a chemist and nano scientist, was also recruited by China's Thousand Talents Program. He was later arrested on January 28, 2020, by the FBI for working for the Chinese government between 2012 and 2017. Lieber was paid $50,000 a month in addition to living expenses to set up a lab at the Wuhan University of Technology. Lieber's specialized field in nanoscience and nanotechnology deals with the controlled manipulation of molecular and genetic structures similar to the concepts applied

---

[58] Hamilton & Ohlberg, *Hidden Hand*, 151.

to GOF research with bioengineering. Lieber failed to make a disclosure of his links to Wuhan in what was called the "WUT-Harvard Joint Nano Key Laboratory" to the Harvard administration. Before this incident, the Chinese Communist Party had honored Lieberman with a "Friendship Award" in 2009. Lieberman's work with Wuhan was only the tip of the iceberg as other trails of funding and collaboration between the NIH and an organization known as the EcoHealth Alliance would be revealed. The EcoHealth Alliance is a non-profit organization that focuses research on SARS-CoV-2 along with emerging health threats such as the Nipah virus and has a collaborative relationship with WIV. Recall our discussion in the previous chapter regarding category C genetically engineered bio agents and the Nipah virus – this will play an important role in reviewing the connections between NIH, EcoHealth, and the WIV in relation to our bioweapon hypothesis in the next chapter.

The 2019 Military World Games: Precursor to a Super-Spreader Event?

As I was in the final stages of writing this book, the 2022 Winter Olympic Games in Beijing were well underway. Although many American conservatives raised concerns about participating in the

Olympics because of China's human rights atrocities, millions of dollars from American corporations sponsored their advertising for the games. These big corporate giants like Coca-Cola, Toyota, Visa, and Intel have spent more than $6.2 million dollars in lobbying for their special interests. Coca-Cola invested over $3 billion dollars in a joint venture with China to sponsor summer and winter Olympic games through 2032.[59] Around the time when many athletes began complaining of the spartan living accommodations and the poor amenities as well as the draconian isolation and lock-down measures that they experienced, House Speaker Nancy Pelosi issued a strong warning to American athletes to comply with the Chinese government. Pelosi told the American athletes: "You're there to compete, do not risk incurring the anger of the Chinese government."[60] With all the coverage given to put spotlight on Beijing's 2022 winter Olympics, another athletic event of international significance had occurred a mere three years prior.

The CCP Ministry of Defense of the People's Republic of China organized the 2019 Military World Games in Wuhan. The games hosted over nine thousand athletes from 109 countries and included over 200,000 volunteers. These athletes represented military servicemen from around the world during October 18 – 27, 2019 just a mere two months prior to any news reports of outbreaks in Wuhan. Given the long incubation period for COVID infections, such a mass event would have the potential to deploy human bioweapon carriers all over the globe. Being that the event is so close to the earliest known occurrences of the virus in November of 2019, brings a level of suspicion to the forefront of speculation. Even if the Wuhan lab did not intentionally release SARS-CoV, an accidental lab leak during the military

[59] Anna Massoglia, *Beijing Winter Olympic's Corporate Sponsors are also Big Lobbying Spenders*, February 3, 2002. Open Secrets – Following Money in Politics. https://www.opensecrets.org/news/2022/02/beijing-winter-olympics-corporate-sponsors-are-also-big-lobbying-spenders/

[60] Daniel Victor, Steven Lee Myers, & Alan Blinder, *Pelosi Warns U.S. Athletes Not to Anger China's Government with Protests*, February 4, 2022. The New York Times.

games would be a disastrous super spreader incident given the timing of the gathering of so many military game participants in one location. Another interesting coincidence is that just a month prior to the military games there was large-scale military exercise conducted by the Chinese government on September 18, 2019. The military exercise was conducted at the Wuhan airport and consisted of a SARS/Coronavirus epidemic scenario that included training for epidemiological investigations, medical investigations, and quarantine drills.[61] According to Markson former PLA military officer and defector Wei Jingsheng also mentioned that an intentional release of coronavirus during the military games as part of a bioweapon test is plausible given the fact that the CCP has been driven to develop an ambitious germ warfare program since 1949. The possibility that SARS-CoV could have originated as a bioweapon during the 2019 military games is not merely a far-fetched speculation. In the August 2021 investigative report to the House Foreign Affairs Committee developed by Congressman Michael T. McCaul there are several compelling facts on the Wuhan Lab and the military games in the report's executive summary[62]:

- The WIV's virus sample database with over 22,000 entries was removed without explanation during the night of September 12, 2019, without explanation (6 days before the Wuhan military exercise). The WIV directors claimed that the database was taken offline for security reasons due to cyber-attacks.

- Dozens of athletes who participated in the military games became sick with COVID like symptoms shortly after they returned to their home countries.

---

[61] Markson, *What Really Happened in Wuhan*, 296-297.

[62] *The Origins of COVID-19: An Investigation of the Wuhan Institute of Virology.* Executive Summary.

- Satellite imagery of Wuhan in September and October 2019 showed a significant uptick in the number of people at local hospitals surrounding the WIV headquarters also with COVID symptoms.

- The People's Liberation Army (PLA) installed one of their chief bioweapon experts, General Chen Wei over the WIV BSL-4 lab in early 2019. Gen. Wei is a researcher at the Academy of Military Sciences in Beijing and a member of the 13th National Committee of the CCP Political Consultative Conference which is one of the party's highest-level decision-making authorities.

On June 21, 2021, Congressman Mike Gallagher in a letter to the Secretary of Defense and the Chairman Joint Chiefs of Staff also raised concerns over the 2019 military games and the WIV:

> From October 18-28, 2019, the World Military Games took place in Wuhan, China. The games featured competitors from over 100 countries, including American athletes and staff. After the games, athletes from several nations reported becoming sick with symptoms they later recognized as consistent with COVID-19. For example, French pentathlete Elodie Clouvel reported becoming sick at the games and later was told by a military doctor that she may have contracted COVID-19. Reports also indicate that athletes from Italy, Germany, Sweden, and Luxembourg may all have become sick with symptoms consistent with COVID-19 at the games. One athlete from Luxembourg reported "nearly empty" streets in Wuhan during the games, recalling, "It was a ghost town" and "there were rumors that the government warned inhabitants not to go out." While anecdotal, these reports raise important questions about

the timeline of the initial COVID-19 outbreak in Wuhan. While the Chinese government first reported an unexplained illness in Wuhan in late December 2019, information released by the U.S. Department of State suggests that lab researchers at the Wuhan Institute of Virology (WIV) became sick with symptoms consistent with COVID-19 in fall 2019 before the established beginning of the outbreak. Subsequent reporting has revealed that three researchers from the WIV sought hospital care for COVID-like symptoms in November 2019. Additionally, former Centers for Disease Control and Prevention Director Robert Redfield has publicly estimated that the virus began circulating in Wuhan in September or October 2019 and new evidence suggests that COVID -19 may have been present in the U.S. as early as December 2019.[63]

Gallagher's letter that was written with the purpose of directing concerns to the Secretary of Defense in the interest of our national security regarding the origin of SARS-CoV raises several questions: (1) Since those who were infected were military athletes from around the world, could the PLA intentionally targeted service personnel as part of an offensive attack?, (2) If the earliest SARS-CoV-2 infections occurred in October, why did the CCP not report any cases to WHO until late December? (3) If U.S. military personnel were asymptomatic when they returned to their stateside installations in October and November, could there have been spread far ahead of any travel bans? In addition to the WIV virus database being taken offline, Markson mentions that satellite data shows a mobile phone blackout surrounding the

---

[63] Letter to the Honorable Lloyd J. Austin III and Gen. Mark A Milley; Congress of the U.S. House of Representatives, Mike Gallagher, June 21, 2021. Site accessed December 3, 2021 from https://gallagher.house.gov/ sites/gallagher.house.gov/ files/Letter_World%20Military%20Games_6.21.pdf.

WIV compound between October 11th and 19th in addition to substantial traffic closures and roadblocks surrounding the area.[64] Ironically months later into the pandemic in 2020 the deputy director of the Chinese Ministry of Foreign Affairs Information Department, Zhao Lijian would allege that it was the U.S. that was responsible for bringing the virus to Wuhan during the military games.[65] The state-controlled CCP propaganda television network began broadcasting this accusation that the U.S. was at fault for introducing the virus and Twitter accounts also began spreading the name of a service member stationed at the bioweapons lab in Fort Detrick, Maryland as the one who was responsible for unleashing the virus in China. This was believed to be China's retaliation upon Trump who was candidly making references to either the "China Virus" or the "Chinese Virus."

As Wuhan Goes Dark a Deadly "Mystery Virus" Emerges

Following the 2019 Military Games in Wuhan the secrecy of the People's Republic of China (PRC) regarding the outbreak in their own backyard held steadfast for nearly three months before the world even had a clue of what was going on. During the outbreak while China was downplaying the severity of the virus photos and videos were circulating showing that Wuhan was being completely locked down and with the hospitals overflowing their capacity, they also began rapidly constructing emergency hospital facilities. Would the unfolding of the pandemic have been different if we had some advance warning before the outbreak was spinning out of control in Wuhan? When reports of a strange SARS like pneumonia was infecting hundreds of people in Wuhan came out, it was not until late December 2019. Not even the World Health Organization (WHO) was notified in the early

---

[64] Markson, *What Really Happened in Wuhan?*, 349.

[65] Yasmeen Abutalem and Damian Paletta, *Nightmare Scenario; Inside the Trump Administration's Response to the Pandemic That Changed the World*, (New York, NY: Harper Collins, 2021), 190-191.

stages. International and domestic flights were running every day out of China's airports during this time. Why the reason for the secrecy? I believe that if SARS-CoV-2 was either accidental or intentional the CCP was doing everything in its power to suppress that information from getting out to the international community. Given the rapid transmission of the virus among local populations and China's open travel even after the military games, SARS-CoV-2 would spread around the world in a matter of weeks. When the U.S. and other nations offered assistance to China to help contain the virus and to investigate its origins, they rejected any help and downplayed the seriousness of the outbreak significantly.

Congressman McCaul's investigative report mentions that the Wuhan lab is strictly controlled by the CCP's "Propaganda Ministry" that has offices in the WIV and during the black-out in the months of October, November and December 2019 they deliberately perpetrated the following acts of information suppression: web sites were scrubbed, lab samples were destroyed, doctors who spoke about the outbreak were either disciplined or silenced and journalists who dared to speak out "disappeared" without a trace.[66] Any public information regarding the outbreak in Wuhan was under an ironclad enforcement by the Communist government. CCP's intentional cover-up kept the virus in Wuhan secretive until the outbreak was raging out of control and the world was soon in the grasps of a deadly pandemic. The Heritage Foundation in its 2021 China Transparency Report describes this costly cover-up as follows:

The COVID-19 pandemic has been one of the most devastating global crises of our time. With millions of lives lost and unprecedented economic devastation, there are many questions that must be answered to ensure that such a tragedy never happens again. But we cannot get those answers without greater transparency from the China where the virus originated. The Chinese government, under

---

[66] *The Origins of COVID-19: An Investigation of the Wuhan Institute of Virology.* Executive Summary, 6.

the governance of the Chinese Communist Party (CCP), neglected its duty to the safety of its own people, and to the world, in its handling of the pandemic. The CCP must be held accountable, and for the sake of those millions of lives, the world needs greater insight into what happened.[67]

> The CCP in step with its Communist authoritarian doctrine is an expert in the suppression of truth for the benefit of the state and this was masterfully orchestrated during the initial pandemic and continues to this day. A U.S. Embassy fact sheet also comments about this apparent and deliberate deception: "the Chinese Communist Party (CCP) has systematically prevented a transparent and thorough investigation of the COVID-19 pandemic's origin, choosing instead to devote enormous resources to deceit and disinformation."[68] This fact sheets further makes disclosure that several researchers inside the WIV became sick in autumn 2019 with COVID symptoms before any reports were made public. It is added that the CCP prevented any interview of these researchers at the WIV.

China's Web of Subversion – the United Nations

Around the time that the WIV virus databases had been taken offline in October 2019, intelligence geospatial analysis revealed a substantial increase in vehicle traffic to local hospitals in Wuhan. Five of six of the Wuhan hospitals had the highest relative volume of traffic

---

[67] Walter Lohman and Justin Rhee, *2021 China Transparency Report*, (Washington, DC: The Heritage Foundation, 2021), Preface, ix.

[68] U.S. Embassy Tbilisi in Georgia. Site accessed June 21, 2021 at https://ge.usembassy.gov/ fact-sheet-activity-at-the-wuhan-institute-of-virology/

in September and October 2019.[69] During this time there was a peak in the local internet search engines of COVID like symptoms. Also, the transit lines within 6.5 miles of the WIV headquarters had a significant increase in traffic. It was evident that there was something happening in Wuhan to increase the number of hospitalizations and personnel traffic to the WIV during Wuhan's black-out. However, by the time that the news of a viral outbreak in Wuhan could no longer be kept under wraps at the end of December 2019 and the beginning of January 2020 the virus had already begun spreading globally. An investigation was needed was needed to quickly determine the origins of the virus if successful steps toward its mitigation were to be implemented quickly. China's cover up significantly delayed any attempt to implement serious epidemiological investigation early on into the outbreak. Everyone's eyes were upon the World Health Organization (WHO) at this time to see what course of action would be taken as they typically address emerging health threats and outbreaks around the globe. Unfortunately, not only was there significant delay in taking any immediate action by the WHO but even when they entered an investigational process, there was absolute failure from the very beginning to produce any worthwhile evidence or relevant data. However, this failure cannot be blamed on the WHO's ineptness or even China's lack of transparency. WHO has significant ties with the CCP.

To further understand the WHO's relationship to China, we need to consider the agency's development and history within the United Nations (U.N.). Not only is this section important for understanding WHO's role with China and the COVID pandemic, but it is also essential in laying the groundwork that will be discussed in further detail in the sixth chapter that deals with the primary reason behind the weaponization of COVID – the global reset agenda. The UN's early development can be attributed to its progenitor organization the League of Nations that came about as a vision of President Woodrow

---

[69] *The Origins of COVID-19: An Investigation of the Wuhan Institute of Virology*, 24-26.

Wilson after the first World War. The League of Nations held to aspirations of achieving world peace through the international cooperation of modern industrialized nations. The League that was formed in 1920 had a significant hurdle to overcome in its day – the Russian Revolution in 1917 that spawned the raw force of the Communist military state was a hostile power to be reckoned with. The only peace that the Soviet Union and the People's Republic of China would agree to was peace by global domination which was a closely held dogma of the Communist Manifesto. The United States as a free constitutional republic never consented to joining the League of Nations because they were unwilling to relinquish national sovereignty at the cost of peace at any price. By the time that international conflicts with the second World War came upon the scene, the League's ideological house of cards came tumbling down and it ceased to exist after only twenty-six years of existence.

With the arrival of the second World War and the demise of the League of Nations, Franklin Roosevelt and Winston Churchill made another attempt to revive the pursuit of international peace. This time beginning with the "Allied Big Four" also known as the "Four Policeman" the four predominant superpower nations were to form the backbone of a new international organization: United States, United Kingdom, Russian and China. Later in 1945 the official Declaration of the United Nations was drafted to restore global civil order at the end of the second World War. However, because of cold war tensions between the U.S. and USSR, American loyalty to the U.N. was not as fervent. This attitude was further exacerbated when Alger Hiss a U.S. State Department official who had been extensively involved with the support and the development of the U.N. went on trial for espionage with accusations of spying for the Soviets.[70]

At the risk of political oversimplification, I would add that most American constitutional conservatives have maintained suspicions

---

[70] James Burnham, *The Web of Subversion* (Belmont, MA: Americanist Library, 1954), 117-118.

of U.N. ambivalence toward communist nations and are reluctant to relinquish national sovereignty for international control. Liberals or progressives on the other hand have been more congenial towards the globalist agenda of the U.N. and see compliance with political systems such as Socialism or Communism as a reasonable means for achieving peaceful democracy. We will provide further discussion on this topic in chapter six. For now, it is sufficient to say that the COVID pandemic has provided an opportunity for global elitist and leftist progressives to implement control measures through fear and subversion. This runs against the values of our constitutional republic when we relinquish our inalienable rights to overreaching government control (i.e., forced closures, mask, and vaccine mandates, etc.). Let me be clear, I am not an "anti-vaxer." While I may not agree with the safety and the efficacy of the COVID vaccine or the claims behind mask wearing, it is the right of the American people to choose whether to be vaccinated or to even wear a mask. Our constitutional liberties guarantee the right to reject the vaccine based on our personal philosophical, religious, spiritual or ideological values. The government does not need to decide these things for us. I believe that it is not constitutional to mandate any of these things especially when people are losing their jobs because of noncompliance and the mandate issue has become a politicized tool for those who seek to impose government control. This plays along with the global agenda of the left and progressives. Government control and more of it is the rallying cry of these global elites and the pandemic is their catalyst for achieving their goals. Global agencies such as the U.N. and the WHO that are sympathetic to Socialist agendas have utilized the COVID crisis as a convenient propaganda platform.

Therefore, it is no surprise that the U.N. and the WHO play into China's agenda for global domination and control. In 2018 at the Central Foreign Affairs Conference, Xi Jinping asserted that China would lead the world's reform of a global governance system. According to Clive Hamilton and Mareike Ohlberg, who are experts on CCP: "The more forthright language reflects Beijing's increasingly robust efforts to reshape international institutions and global regimes to suit CCP's interests...the CCP wants China to be seen as a *protector* of multi-lateral institutions, presenting itself as a much-needed counterweight to 'US unilateralism'.[71] Multilateralism is a precept of the U.N. which encourages nations to be inclusive in matters such as international trade and commerce where all nations are given equal opportunity. At the 2018 United Nations General Assembly, foreign minister Wang Yi called China a "champion of multilateralism."

This was given full support by the U.N. delegates and recognized as common ground for supporting multilateralism which was also readily endorsed by the European Union. The *modus operandi* of the CCP is to strengthen its position in large multilateral institutions such as the U.N. while always coming out as the stronger party. Because China is skilled at using the language favored by globalists such as "a community of shared future for mankind" they are given favorable status in the U.N. China has used its position in the U.N. to become a permanent member of their Security Council and has been aggressively expanding its influence throughout the world. Therefore, China has been able to assert itself into countries like Afghanistan after U.S. troop withdrawal for building highways and infrastructure to exercise its claim on natural resources. Four principal U.N. agencies are run by Chinese Nationals: Food & Agriculture, International Telecommunications, International Aviation, and Industrial Development with the purpose of gaining a global advantage. The U.N. praises China for being a leader in "economic growth and an important catalyst for sustainable economic goals" while saying absolutely nothing about the CCP's human rights violations and its brutal oppressive regime."[72]

---

[71] Hamilton & Ohlberg, *Hidden Hand*, 249.

[72] Hamilton & Ohlberg, *Hidden Hand*, 251-252.

Muddied Waters – The WHO, China's Global Pawn

China also has a history of considerable influence with the U.N.'s WHO that goes back to its early development. In the 1930's Dr. Szeming Sze from the People's Republic of China established himself as a distinguished physician and studied at Cambridge. Sze served as Chinese ambassador to Great Britain and later the U.S. and served on the U.N.'s Economic and Social Council. Sze's single greatest ambition was to create an international public health organization within the U.N., and he was assisted directly by Alger Hiss who we previously mentioned as being tried by the U.S. for espionage and spying for the Soviets. The two of them planned a draft resolution over dinner and soon the World Health Organization was developed just a few years after the creation of the U.N. To this day the WHO and CCP have very close ties as China is the largest contributor to its annual $7.2 billion budget with its annual giving increasing by 52%. This is followed by the Bill and Melinda Gates Foundation with a $531 million annual contribution.[73] The U.S. was the third largest contributor to WHO at $400 mil-

---

[73] Srinivas Mazumdaru, DW Asia April 17, 2020, *What Influence Does China Have Over the WHO?*, Site accessed December 8, 2021 from https://www.dw.com/ en/ what-influence-does-china-have-over-the-who/a-53161220

lion in 2017 until the Trump Administration called to defund them for being too soft on China's handling of COVID.[74] WHO funding was quickly restated under the Biden Administration. The current Director of WHO Tedros Adhanom has a long-standing friendship with China's President Jinping. Tedros was the former minister of health and foreign affairs in Ethiopia but is also a member of the nation's Communist Party known as the Tigray People's Liberation Front in Africa that is recognized as a radical paramilitary group that has been branded as a terrorist organization by other African nations. Just before Tedros was elected as the WHO Director he was an honored guest speaker at Peking University. As soon as he was installed into the WHO directorship, Tedros made statements to the Chinese state media that he and WHO would support the "One China" principle recognizing Beijing as the legitimate Chinese government. Also, WHO's Chief of Staff Bernhard Schwartlander led a delegation to the Belt and Road Forum for health project cooperation with China.[75] Recall that the Belt and Road Initiative (BRI) is the CCP's infrastructure program that is a vehicle for global domination. The WHO is in full endorsement of the BRI.

When the COVID pandemic was raging out of control in Wuhan in January 2020 the WHO was not expedient in taking immediate action to mitigate the virus in China or to issue emergency warnings internationally. In mid-January 2020 the WHO along with China significantly downplayed the COVID outbreak and tweeted that it was closely following the PRC's investigation which claimed that "there was no clear evidence of human-to-human transmission."[76] The WHO also claimed that spread of

---

[74] Adam Shaw, *Calls Escalate for WHO to be Defunded Over China Ties, Coronavirus Response*. Fox News April 8, 2020. Site accessed December 8, 2021 from https://www.foxnews.com/politics / who-defunded-china-ties-coronavirus-response

[75] Markson, *What Really Happened in Wuhan*, 146-147.

[76] Brahma Chellaney, *The World Health Organization Must Stop Covering Up China's Mistakes*, April 23, 2020. *The Project Syndicate*. Source Accessed December 8, 2021 from https://www.marketwatch.com/story/ the-who-has-a-big-china-problem-2020-04-2.

transmission from asymptomatic infected individuals was not a concern and discouraged testing. At the same time China began mass stockpiling of Personal Protective Equipment (PPE) and other medical equipment which it had been acquiring for weeks causing mass shortages in hospitals around the world. Tedros met with President Xi on January 28, 2019 and praised China for their handling of the outbreak which he attributed to the leadership of President Xi. A WHO team of twelve members were sent to Wuhan but this may have been nothing more than PR as none of them were granted direct access to the WIV lab. Tedros's inaction stands as a contrast to the former WHO director Brundtland who quickly initiated travel restrictions from the China during the 2003 SARS outbreak.[77] By February 2020 there were 70,000 cases and 2,500 deaths and while Tedros admitted to a public health emergency in China there was not an official pandemic declaration until March. In Washington tempers were flaring up over how WHO was not addressing the lack of transparency in China. Sen. Marco Rubio, R-Florida stated: "The Chinese Communist Party used the WHO to mislead the world. The organization's leadership is either complicit or dangerously incompetent. I will work with the Trump administration to ensure the WHO is independent and has not been compromised by the CCP before we continue our current funding.[78]" The WHO literally stalled out any chance of a serious investigation of China regarding the virus. This is especially evident when the U.S. Ambassador to Geneva Andrew Bremberg met with Tedros and Schwartlander for the WHO to request virus samples from China. The meeting dragged out for four hours without any commitment from Tedros to make any demands from China to obtain lab samples.[79] The WIV specializes in lab samples. How difficult would it be to

[77] Michael Collins, *The WHO and China: Dereliction of Duty*, February 27, 2020. Asia Unbound, Council on Foreign Relations. Site accessed December 8, 2021 from https://www.cfr.org/blog/ who-and-china-dereliction-duty

[78] Adam Shaw, *Calls Escalate for WHO to be Defunded Over China Ties, Coronavirus Response.*

[79] Markson, *What Really Happened in Wuhan*, 147.

produce one viable SARS-CoV-2 viral sample and for WHO to make such a reasonable request? Of course, there is much to question especially when files with over 22,000 viral samples at the WIV disappeared in the middle of the night in October 2019. Brett Schaefer who is a senior researcher at the conservative group Heritage Organization pointed out that the WHO's lack of action along with China's lack of transparency have enabled the virus to spread into a lethal global pandemic: "It is now clear that Beijing's response to COVID-19 enabled its spread, to the detriment of public health and economies throughout the world."[80]

China's Zoonotic Scapegoat – The Wet Market Origin Theory

One of the most hotly debated topics for SARS-CoV-2 regards the origin of the virus. Understanding its origin not only helps us in further mitigation but also to take the necessary preparedness planning to either prevent it from happening again and to develop effective countermeasures. The CCP state media was quick to declare that the virus source was the fresh meat markets in Wuhan and they along with the mainstream media have held steadfast to this narrative ever since. This is what is commonly referred to as the "wet market theory" or the "natural origins theory." Considering that outdoor Chinese food markets are traditional sources for seafood and other exotic animals such as bats and pangolins that are regarded as culinary delicacies, the first assumption would be what we call a "zoonotic" disease source which comes from an animal especially when consumed for its meat. China has maintained its position that the virus was transmitted through bats or pangolins sold at the Wuhan markets. As a first glance a zoonotic origin is not an unreasonable hypothesis to consider given that diseases

---

[80] Brett D. Schaeffer, *The World Health Organization Bows to China*; Heritage Foundation Commentary Global Politics, April 28, 2020. Source accessed December 8, 2021 from https://www.heritage.org/global-politics/commentary/the-world-health-organization-bows-china

of an animal origin do account for about two-thirds of human infectious diseases which cause a billion cases of human illness each year.[81] The H1N1 outbreak (swine flu) was passed on from hogs to farmers in Mexico and later the Ebola outbreak in Africa is highly suspected to be related to the consumption of bush meat. Could the Wuhan markets be a source of origin for SARS-CoV-2? One would have expected that the WHO team gave immediate focus upon the local markets and the lab. However, according to Markson when she interviewed WHO spokesperson Margaret Harris the response was: "The focus was of the mission was on learning from the response, not looking at the origin, so the wet market, lab, etc. were not on the agenda."[82] Why would WHO focus upon Wuhan's response protocols when there were other components of far greater importance to evaluate in terms of the lab and market? These items carry much more weight for determining the origin of the virus, yet they were not addressed by the WHO investigation team. Another huge obstacle was that the markets were shut down and completely sanitized and disinfected on January 1, 2020. This destroyed any forensic evidence that could have been collected and analyzed for a viable market origin hypothesis.

In addition to the lack of viral samples obtained from the markets the cave dwelling bats and pangolins are not readily sold in Wuhan. According to Oxford's Wildlife Conservation Fellow, Professor David Macdonald there is no evidence that bats, or pangolins were sold at Wuhan's wet markets between May 2017 and November 2019.[83] This report includes data from a joint research project between Oxford's WildCRU and the China West Normal University, Nanchong, and Hubei

---

[81] *Emerging Diseases from Animals*, 2015 NIH article. Site accessed December 9, 2021 from https://www.ncbi.nlm.nih.gov/ pmc/articles/PMC7124125/

[82] Markson, *What Really Happened in Wuhan*, 84.

[83] Isaac Healey, *Bats and Pangolins Not Sold at Wuhan Markets Says Oxford Research*, The Oxford Student, June 8, 2021. Site accessed December 9, 2021 from https://www.oxfordstudent.com/2021/06/08/bats-and-pangolins-not-sold-at-wuhan-markets-says-oxford-research

University of Traditional Chinese medicine that focused on tick borne diseases in these markets since May 2017. According to Macdonald the research that reviewed 47,381 animals from 38 species including 31 protected species concluded: "Bats are rarely consumed in Central China, where market photos generally depict Indonesia. Pangolin trade is still a significant issue in other Chinese cities and trading nodes, but not in Wuhan." He further adds that the 2002 SARS epidemic that began in Guandong was transmitted by palm civets as an intermediary transferring an infection which began in cave-dwelling horseshoe bats. Macdonald stated that "this had led to the original hypothesis that COVID-19 originated in bats, who are known vectors of coronavirus, and spread through pangolins to people."

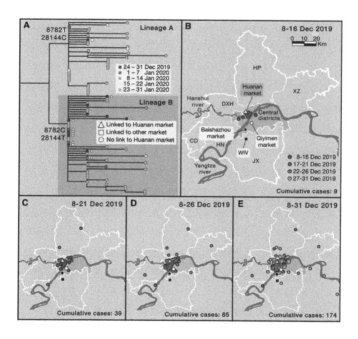

Also, if we look for direct links between confirmed cases who presented at Wuhan hospitals and those who obtained items from the markets the numbers are quite small in comparison. According to the peer reviewed journal *The Lancet* only 27 of the 41 patients had direct exposure to the Huanan Seafood Market.[84] Further findings confirm that the first identified COVID case related to the market was not part of the exposure groups of any COVID cases that were identified later. This data was also reviewed by Jan Cohen in the January 26, 2020 edition of *Science Magazine*:

The first human infections must have occurred in November 2019 – if not earlier – because there is an incubation time between infection and symptoms surfacing. If so, the virus possibly spread silently between people in Wuhan – and perhaps elsewhere – before the cluster of cases from the city's now-infamous Hunan Seafood Wholesale Market was discovered in late December. This virus came into that marketplace before it came out of that marketplace.[85]

Although the Wuhan Health Commission noted that diagnostic tests had confirmed these cases by January 10, 2020, none of the medical admission records mention the market as the source. However, the CCP state media still insist upon the market as the virus origin. Cohen mentions that Kristian Andersen who is an evolutionary biologist after analyzing 2019-nCoV sequences stated: "The scenario of somebody being infected outside the market and then later bringing it to the market is one of the three scenarios we have considered that is still consistent with the data." While there is not any conclusive proof that SARS-CoV-2 has a basis of zoonotic origin with the markets we will see

---

[84] Caolin Huang & Yeming Wang, *Clinical Features of Patients Infected with 2019 Novel Coronavirus in Wuhan China*. The Lancet; Vol. 395 Issue 10223, February 15, 2020.

[85] Jan Cohen, *Wuhan Seafood Market May Not be Source of Novel Virus Spreading Globally: Description of Earliest Cases Suggests Outbreak Began Elsewhere*. January 26, 2020 Science Magazine. Source accessed October 15, 2021 from https://www.science.org/content/article/wuhan-seafood-market-may-not-be-source-novel-virus-spreading-globally.

in the next chapter that there is a link between the GOF research and cave dwelling bats. This will result in somewhat of a "both-and" origin hypothesis not from the markets but from bats with the intent of weaponizing SARS-CoV-2.

CHAPTER 4

A Deadly Virus of Stealth Design

You can engineer a virus without leaving any trace. The answers you are looking for, however, can only be found in the archives of the Wuhan laboratory. – Dr. Ralph Baric, Distinguished Professor of Epidemiology & Microbiology UNC Chapel Hill

An Efficient Bio-Machine

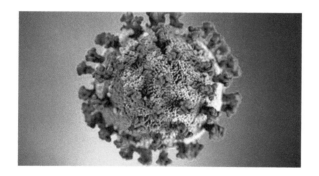

For practical purposes the virus that is referenced in this book is one of the four subclassifications of coronaviruses found in bats and rodents known as a betacoronavirus and is referred to as SARS-CoV-2. It is of the genus that includes SARS (Severe Acute Respiratory Syndrome) and MERS (Middle Eastern Respiratory Syndrome). All of us are quite familiar with the electron microscope photos of the SARS-CoV-2 virus as we have been barraged with constant images across the spectrum of every media source conceivable. The peculiar spike protein structure provided the virus with its name "Coronavirus" from the Latin word *corona* for crown. The Coronavirus family of RNA viruses causes disease in mammals and birds. This spike "crown" is what enables the virus to have a high level of transmission as it attaches to human respiratory cells with its ACE2 receptors. SARS-CoV-2 uses this spike structure to fuse itself with incredible tenacity onto the nose, mouth, and lung membranes where after entry its uncoated genomic RNA is translated into polyproteins. From here it begins a machine-like efficient process of replication with virus-induced double membrane vesicles (DMV's).[86] SARS-CoV-2 is an RNA (ribonucleic acid) based single-stranded molecular structure which permits it to directly code for amino acids and act as a messenger between human DNA (deoxyribonucleic acid) to replicate proteins. Because of what is referred to as the D614 G mutation found in the outer spike protein it can remain highly elusive of conventional medical countermeasures and is difficult to treat. The size of the SARS-CoV-2 is impressive as it is large on a microscopic scale compared to the conventional influenza virus that is a mere 13.5 kilobases (kb) compared to the Coronavirus being 30 kb or 30,000 nucleotides. By definition it is considered a "novel" virus which means that it is a new emerging pathogen previously unknown which there is very little natural immunity until the virus has run its course in the population to achieve what we call "herd immunity." The way that the SARS-CoV-2 virus impacts individuals remains a mystery. Most individuals experience mild cold like symptoms and recover quickly while in others it can develop into a lethal pneumonia. Some may be infected and yet not manifest any symptoms (asymptomatic). Like most novel viruses SARS-CoV-2 also can mutate into genetic variants. For that reason, it can remain in the human population for many years just as H1N1 variants have been circulating since 2009. While the initial emergence of a novel virus is usually adverse the good news is

---

[86] COVID-19 Virology, Biology & Novel Laboratory Diagnosis. Source accessed June 10, 2021, from https://www.ncib.nlm.nih.gov/pmc/articles/PMC7883242

that the morbidity and severity can naturally diminish over time as the human immune system learns to adapt and to become more resilient.

Viral Engineering – Gain of Function Research

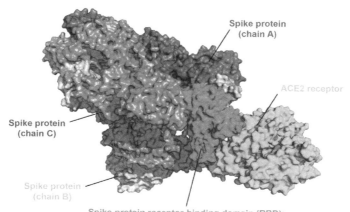

Spike protein receptor-binding domain (RBD): "molecular glue" between virus and surface of lung cells enables SARS-CoV-2 to bind 10-20 times more tightly than SARS-CoV-1

My hypothesis is that SARS-CoV-2 was genetically engineered and modified with enhanced properties to have the unique biological characteristics mentioned above to be used in the deployment of a bioweapon. The type of research that could make genetic engineering possible lies within the realm of Gain of Function research (GOFR). GOFR focuses upon growing generations of microorganisms under conditions that cause mutations in a virus. The lab experiments that involve GOFR use the artificial manipulation of pathogens giving them a "gain of advantage in or through a function such as increased transmissibility."[87] Australian biogenetic researcher Dr. Nikolai Petrovsky focused on this peculiar ACE2 receptor in a supercomputer analysis conducted through the Oracle

---

[87] Mohana Basu, *What is Gain of Function? Research Field Back in Focus as COVID Linked to China Lab Accident.* May 22, 2021. Source accessed July 6, 2021 from https://theprint.in/theprint-essential/what-is-gain-of-function-research-field-back-in-focus-as-covid-linked-to-china-lab-accident/662625/

Corporation. He noted that the properties of SARS-CoV-2 are 10 – 20 times more consolidated in structure than the original SARS spike protein.

The findings of the Dr. Petrovsky's computer analysis concluded that the viral properties are perfectly adapted to human transmission. He stated, "It really looked like this was a virus that was optimally designed to infect humans."[88] GOFR can include genetic engineering where the viral genetic code is modified to achieve a specific purpose. An artificial mand-made virus can be created by joining two or more viral fragments. These are called "Chimeric Viruses." One of the methods used in the genetic engineering of viral strands is known as "Reverse Genetics System" (RGS). RGS can be used to rapidly engineer viruses with desired mutations to study a virus *in vitro* (in an artificial environment such as a test tube outside of a living organism) and *in vivo* (within a live host). The viruses created by RGS processes can also be used for vaccine development research. All of this provides a very basic description of some of the activities undertaken within GOFR.

Scientists who utilize GOFR usually point out that the benefits outweigh the risks for peaceful and humanitarian purposes

---

[88] Markson, *What Really Happened in Wuhan*, 163.

(i.e., advancement of scientific knowledge, discovery of new medical treatments, vaccine development, etc.). However, there is also potential risk for a catastrophic lab accident such as a breach at a BSL-4 facility where a deadly pathogen infects lab staff or leaks out to the surrounding population. This possible scenario is referred to as the "lab leak hypothesis" that includes the possibility that an unintentional incident that may have occurred in Wuhan. Also, while there are ethical guidelines that are specified in such declarations of Dual Use Research of Concern (DURC), intentional adversarial purposes such as the development of military weapons cannot be ruled out as a misuse of GOFR. Bioethics Professor Michael J. Selgelid from Monash University in Melbourne published an intriguing article for the NIH on August 8, 2016, on the ethical dilemma of GOFR. Selgelid begins with a basic definition of GOFR: "Gain-of-function (GOF) research involves experimentation that aims or is expected to (and/or, perhaps, actually does) increase the transmissibility and/or virulence of the pathogens."[89] He goes on explain that while the intended outcome of GOFR is to benefit public health preparedness and medical countermeasures, there are risks: "Despite these important potential benefits, GOFR can pose risks regarding biosecurity and biosafety." Given these inherent risks with GOFR it remains a hotly debated topic regarding the funding of such research from the taxpayer's pockets. The processes for justifying the funding for GOFR have a convoluted history with both the funding and the research being temporarily paused and then reinstated.

A Temporary Pause in GOFR Funding that was Resumed

Selgelid mentions that the potential risks related to biosecurity and biosafety led to the "pause" in 2014 on funding GOFR experiments

---

[89] Michael J. Selgelid, *Gain of Function Research: Ethical Analysis*. National Institute of Health White Paper, June 12, 2016 published with open access at Spingerlink.com.

involving influenza, SARS, and MERS" during the Obama administration. This is the stated purpose of the Ethical Analysis White Paper written by Selgelid that was commissioned by the NIH. His paper points out a controversial GOFR published in 2012 involving "highly pathogenic H5N1 (avian) influenza strains that were transmissible between ferrets" that may have leaked out due to a lab mishap. Selgelid also adds that "Of particular concern in the context of life science research is that advances in biotechnology may enable development and use of a new generation of biological weapons of mass destruction." He cites several other historical GOFR projects involving the use of "experiments with potential implications for biological weapons-making" such as the genetic engineering of a super strain of the mousepox virus in 2001, the artificial syntheses of a live polio virus in 2002, and the reconstruction of the 1918 deadly Spanish Flu by using synthetic genomics in 2005. Selgelid's forty-two-page white paper makes extensive recommendations for promoting an ethical framework for GOFR in light of these dangerous experiments.

The US National Science Advisory Board for Biosecurity (NSABB) then had the responsibility for submitting recommendations to the government on these matters regarding the risks and benefits of GOFR. In May 2016 the NSABB submitted their report for GOFR to the U.S. Government that included seven findings and seven recommendations. The 109-page report is comprehensive and includes most of Professor Selgelid's ethical framework along with a call to strengthen biosecurity and safety. The NSABB report finding number seven addresses funding for projects that are international in scope: "Funding and conducting GOF research of concern encompasses many issues that are international in nature."[90] This finding is a broad-stroke reference to GOFR that implies collaboration between the U.S. and foreign nations. No doubt this caveat provided an open door for

---

[90] *Recommendations for the Evaluation and Oversight of Proposed Gain-of-Function Research*, A Report of the National Science Advisory Board for Biosecurity, May 2016.

GOFR projects in Wuhan. Another reference to the funding of GOFR is included in its second recommendation: "An advisory body that is designed for transparency and public engagement should be utilized as part of the U.S. government's ongoing evaluation of oversight policies for GOF research of concern." Overall, the report presents a positive recommendation for resuming funding for GOFR within the oversight of multidisciplinary organizations.

However, there are no specific corrective actions issued regarding the serious lab breaches with Avian virus or the risky bioweapon research mentioned in the NSABB report. My experience in working with federal and state agencies it that it is a routine practice to conduct an after-action review for such incidents and then to submit a corrective action plan to meet Homeland Security Exercise Evaluation Procedures (HSEEP). However, there is no reference to any HSEEP procedures in the follow up report. It only included a statement on the "Federal-Level Review of Certain GOFR Studies" which refers to a summary from the U.S. Department of Health and Human Services: "Under the *HHS Framework* certain proposals with the potential for generating highly pathogenic avian influenza viruses that are transmissible among mammals by respiratory droplets receive special review and approval before being funded by HHS. This policy was subsequently expanded to include review of similar proposals involving low pathogenic avian influenza H7N9 viruses." The *HHS Framework* referred to in this statement was revised in a 2017 summary titled *Framework for Guiding Funding Decisions about Proposed Research Involving Enhanced Potential Pandemic Pathogens*. The *HHS Framework* is a summary issued for the purpose of addressing the reinstatement of funding for GOFR through what it defines as "PPP's": "The HHS P3CO Framework is intended to guide HHS funding decisions on individual proposed research that is reasonable anticipated to create, transfer, or use enhanced PPP's...*A potential pandemic pathogen (PPP)* is a pathogen that is (1) It is likely highly transmissible and likely capable of wide and uncontrollable spread in human populations. (2) It is likely highly virulent and likely to cause significant morbidity and/or mortality in humans."[91] The HHS summary further states that funding may be allowed for such research as long as it has an "appropriate management of risks" and is "ethically justifiable."

Federal Agency Relationships Supportive of GOFR Funding

The processes for the pause and then the reinstatement of GOFR were not highly publicized in the three years between 2014 and 2017. The federal agencies who were providing oversight of GOFR funding managed to maintain a low profile within the public health and medical sector because of their existing relationships with the HHS, CDC, FDA, and NIH. It is easy for things to get lost in the smoke and mirror transactions of Washington bureaucrats without much public attention especially when closely knit federal agencies have vetted interests in their pet projects. When the funding for GOFR was put on pause in 2014 the federal advisory committee that was called upon to provide initial oversight was the NSABB since it is responsible for matters pertaining to biosafety and biosecurity. The NSABB is made up of a panel of subject matter experts that reports directly to the U.S. Department of Health and Human Services (HHS). Other significant agencies within HHS are the Centers for Disease Control and Prevention (CDC), the Food and Drug Administration (FDA – who grants authorization for vaccines and medical countermeasures), and the National Institutes of Health. All these agencies are closely related, and all share funding streams for their programs. The NIH with its role in biomedical research was assigned to the deliberative processes for the evaluation of GOFR funding especially within the scope of its White Paper. After the NSABB report was published then the HHS issued its *Framework for Guiding Funding Decisions* for GOFR.

---

[91] *Framework for Guiding Funding Decisions about Proposed Research Involving Enhanced Potential Pandemic Pathogens*, 2017 U.S. Department of Health & Human Services.

After three years of reporting process within HHS, NIH, and the NSABB came the recommendation to reinstate funding for GOFR. On May 17, 2017, Francis Collins, Director of NIH, and Anthony Fauci who was at the time with the National Institute of Allergy and Infectious Diseases along with other federal health and medical agencies provided testimony before the House Appropriations Subcommittee. The testimony given was on the "Transformative Power of Biomedical Research" which was filled with glowing tribute to its humanitarian benefits to include notable advances such in cancer research and medical treatment. Some of the testimony highlights included the following points[92]:

- Finding new treatments thus requires NIH to play a lead role – by investing in the early stages of therapeutic development to "de-risk" such projects.

- The core of our mission remains basic biomedical science. Given the exploratory and, hence, unpredictable nature of fundamental discovery, basic science is generally not supported in the private sector – but it provides the critical foundation for advances in disease diagnosis, treatment, and prevention through future clinical applications.

- As a current example, the emergence of "cryo-EM," a new form of electron microscopy, has dramatically sped up the time needed to visualize the exquisite details of biological structures including protein-protein and protein-drug complexes.

---

[92] NIH Director Press Release, *Testimony on the Transformative Power of Biomedical Research*; Witness appearing before the House Appropriations Subcommittee on Labor, HHS, Education, and Related Agencies. May 17, 2017. Source Accessed on December 13, 2021 from https://www.nih.gov/about-nih / who-we-are/nih-director/testimony-transformative-power-biomedical-research.

- If America is to continue its global leadership in biomedicine, we need to be sure this next generation has the confidence that there will be support for them. This is a priority for me.

The language given within the hearing testimony was quite a tribute to medical advances in cancer research with no reference to the biosecurity risks of GOFR. Who would argue with such a glowing report of humanitarian research? Just four months later the NIH Director Gary Collins published their press release: *NIH Lifts Funding Pause on Gain-of-Function Research*:

Today the National Institutes of Health announced that it is lifting a funding pause dating back to October 2014 on gain-of-function (GOF) experiments involving influenza, SARS, and MERS viruses. GOF research is important in helping us identify, understand, and develop strategies and effective countermeasures against rapidly evolving pathogens that pose a threat to public health. The funding pause was lifted in response to today's release of the *Department of Health and Human Services Framework for Guiding Funding Decisions about Proposed Research Involving Enhanced Potential Pandemic Pathogens.*"[93]

> With the green light for continued funding of GOFR projects, taxpayers were not aware that their dollars were going to make the way for a lethal pandemic to be unleashed over the next two years.

---

[93] NIH Director Announcement, *NIH Lifts Funding Pause on Gain-of-Function Research*, December 19, 2017. Accessed source on December 13, 2021 from https://www.nih.gov/about-nih/who-we-are/nih-director/statements/nih-lifts-funding-pause-gain-function-research.

Funding Sources for GOFR Come to Light

According to Sharri Markson and her investigative team, U.S. Diplomat Rick Switzer who was assigned to the U.S. Embassy in Beijing and Jamie Fouss the U.S. Consul-General to Wuhan raised concerns about their visit to inspect the WIV.[94] Switzer sent an unclassified cable to the U.S. State Department about the poor safety practices in Wuhan's BSL-4 lab and their handling of lethal viral pathogens. Switzer's cable also provided details on a database of deadly viral pathogens capable of starting a global pandemic which were under the WIV's Global Virome Project (GVP). Switzer's cable also mentions the Wuhan GVP research on animal-based diseases in partnership with the EcoHealth Alliance and with the NIH. Markson adds:

The cable also makes clear the extent of the United States involvement in with the Wuhan Institute of Virology. "In the last year, the institute has also hosted visits from the National Institutes of Health (NIH), National Science Foundation and experts from the University of Texas Medical Branch in Galveston." It said that the Galveston branch had trained the Wuhan lab technicians in lab management and maintenance while the US National Science Foundation had just concluded a workshop with the Wuhan Institute in Shenzhen involving 40 scientists from the United States and China.[95]

Markson's investigative findings provide us with a startling revelation that prior to the pandemic there was funding of the Wuhan lab by the NIH along with the National Science Foundation of China. Not only was there funding of the Wuhan lab but they were also training China's scientists. There are emails that recently surfaced sent from Dr. Shi Zhengli the Senior Scientist & Professor of the Wuhan Lab to Ralph Baric who is a microbiology professor at the University

---

[94] Markson, *What Really Happened in Wuhan*, 127-135.
[95] Ibid, 130.

of North Carolina.[96] Zhengli refers to her meeting with Baric at UT Medical Branch in Galveston and summarizes an invitation for him to attend a symposium on "Emerging Viral Diseases" in Wuhan; she adds: "According to your agenda, we set out meeting date from 20-22nd October, 2018, immediately after your meeting in Hong Kong. Your local cost and travel between Hong Kong and Wuhan will be covered by our meeting sponsor." What is significant about this email exchange that occurred in February 2018 between Zhengli known as the "bat woman" for her expertise in bat zoonotic research and Professor Baric from UNC is the scope of research that they were working on at the time related to coronaviruses in bats.

USAID is a federal U.S. agency that administers civilian foreign aid and development assistance; it has a budget over $27 billion. The federal agency not only provided funding for the Wuhan lab and other global projects, but they are also an active part of the Biden

---

[96] Glenn Beck, *Crimes or Cover-Up? Research*, November 2021.

administration's international Climate Initiative.[97] According to Robert F. Kennedy, Jr. there is another disturbing revelation concerning USAID's funding for GOFR: "Military planners at the Pentagon, BARDA (*Biomedical Advanced Research & Development Authority*), DARPA (*Defense Advanced Research Projects Agency*), and the CIA (through USAID) began pouring money into 'gain-of-function" experiments' (*italics in parenthesis added for definition of acronyms*)."[98] Kennedy later adds his comment regarding this strange relationship that the CIA's reputation internationally with power and control especially with the covert subversion of governments: "The CIA does not do public health...The CIA does coups d'état." The CIA's historical preoccupations have been power and control...The CIA does not do public health. It does not do democracy. The CIA does coups d'état."[99]

Markson claims that the information cable that Switzer sent to the U.S. State Department about the funding from NIH and EcoHealth went unnoticed until Pompeo initiated an investigation of the Wuhan lab in early 2020. However, the mainstream media quickly dismissed it as a conspiracy theory that was associated with the Trump administration saying that it lacked any genuine credibility. In the midst of these so-called conspiracy theory accusations, there is proof that high-risk viral pathogen GOFR was going on in American universities several years prior to the pandemic. On November of 2015 the University of North Carolina published an article titled, *New SARS-Like Virus Can Jump Directly from Bats to Humans, No Treatment Available*. The article which cited researchers at Wuhan stated:

---

[97] USAID Press Release: *USAID Announces Robust Targets to Advance President Biden's Prepare Climate Initiative*, November 1, 2021. Source obtained November 10, 2021, from USAID site: https://www.usaid.gov/news-information/press-releases/nov-1-2021-usaid-announces-robust-targets-advance-president-biden-prepare-climate-initiative.

[98] Robert F. Kennedy, Jr., *The Real Anthony Fauci: Bill Gates, Big Pharma and the Global War on Democracy & Public Health*, (New York, NY: Skyhorse Publishing, 2021), 800.

[99] Kennedy, *The Real Anthony Fauci*, 800.

Baric and his team demonstrated that the newly-identified SARS-like virus, labeled SHC014-CoV and found in the Chinese horseshoe bats, can jump between bats and humans by showing that the virus can latch onto and use the same human and bat receptor for entry. The virus also replicates as well as SARS-CoV in primary human lung cells, the preferred target for infection.[100]

Very early on research was being conducted with ancestral viruses closely related to SARS-CoV-2. There is mounting evidence for the funding of GOF research in collaboration with Wuhan prior to the pandemic.

Although there was a pause put on GOFR funding in 2014, Congressman Guy Reschenthaler (R-PA) uncovered $1.1 million in Obama-era funding to Wuhan through the EcoHealth Alliance that was awarded through USAID.[101] Even more recently Reschenthaler revealed a $4.7 million dollar grant to EcoHealth from USAIDUSAID earmarked for projects described as "overseas foreign assistance pro-grams." This prompted a letter drafted by Reschenthaler and twen-ty-five other House Republicans to USAID Administrator Samantha Power requiring that she give an account for involvement with GOFR projects with Wuhan.[102] Power a former UN Ambassador and U.S. State Department transition team member under Obama was appointed by Biden to head USAID in January 2021. USAID developed the "PREDICT" Project in 2009 to advance preparedness planning for

---

[100] Science Daily, November 10, 2015. *New SARS-Like Virus Can Jump Directly from Bats to Humans, No Treatment Available.* University of North Carolina at Chapel Hill. Source accessed July 6, 2021, from https://www.sciencedaily.com/releases/2015/11/151110115711.htm.

[101] Guy Lorin Reschenthaler, 14th Congressional District Press Release, May 14, 2021. *$1.1 Million in Taxpayer Funding Sent to the Wuhan Institute of Technology.* Site accessed on December 13, 2021 from https://reschenthaler.house.gov/media/press-releases/reschenthaler-uncovers-11-million-taxpayer-funding-sent-wuhan-institute.

[102] Congressional Letter, February 7, 2022 to the Honorable Samantha Power regarding USAID funding to EcoHealth.

"emerging pandemic threat" to include developing diagnostic capabilities for coronaviruses.[103] This project is well funded and partners with EcoHealth for international research specifically for "high consequence and dangerous pathogens" arising from zoonotic sources with the potential of developing into pandemics. Another $600,000 was also granted to Wuhan from EcoHealth through grants from the National Institute of Allergy and Infectious Disease where Fauci was a director. Although Fauci has denied that GOFR was being funded in Wuhan, emails have been released to the public that refer to a PDF attachment with the description *SARS Gain of function* and Dr. Zhengli is mentioned in the attachment description.[104] The emails that were sent from Fauci's iPad during the early phases of the pandemic on February 1, 2020 to various individuals in the NIH states: "The paper you sent me says the experiments were performed before the gain of function pause but have since been reviewed and approved by the NIH." In the emails Fauci also requested that there be a conference call that needed to be "in total confidence." In spite of Fauci's denials, the NIH came to the forefront and actually released an article updated on October 20, 2021 stating that there were research grants that were approved for the research in Wuhan: "The research that NIH approved under the EcoHealth Alliance with a subaward to the Wuhan Institute of Virology in Wuhan, China sought to understand how animal coronaviruses, especially bat coronaviruses, evolve naturally in the environment and have the potential to become transmissible to the human population."[105] This was addressed directly by Senator Rand Paul during a Senate Health, Education, Labor, and Pensions Committee hearing on Thursday, November 4, 2021. Paul in a strong statement to

---

[103] PREDICT Project Site, USAID. Source accessed on June 9, 2021 from https://ohi.vetmeducdavids.edu/programs- projects/predict-project.

[104] Glenn Beck, *Crimes or Cover-Up? Research*

[105] National Institute of Allergy and Infectious Diseases, *SARS-CoV-2 and NIAID – supported Bat Coronavirus Research*, site accessed on December 16, 2021 from https://www.niaid.nih.gov/diseases conditions/coronavirus-bat-research.

Fauci remarked: "Dr. Fauci, I don't expect you today to admit that you approved of NIH funding for a gain of function research in Wuhan, but your repeated denials have worn thin...The facts are clear. The NIH did fund gain of function research in Wuhan despite your protestations."[106] The hearing does bring to light the fact that GOFR project collaboration with China through NIH and EcoHealth has been going on for some time now. Both Collins and Fauci on behalf of the NIH presented the case before the House Appropriations Subcommittee in 2017 that GOFR was for the benefit of making advancements in medical science. In addition to the emails that have been released there is further evidence that a lab origins hypothesis was deliberately suppressed by Fauci and Collins. A virologist by the name of Dr. Kristian Andersen with Scripps Lab which specializes in engineered recombinant protein development research, told Fauci that the SARS-CoV-2 has possible engineered components and that the "genome is inconsistent with expectations form evolutionary theory."[107] We are told that the conference calls and emails were specifically for the purpose of suppressing the truth about a lab origins hypothesis. Fauci and Collins have since held to their zoonotic origin narrative and that GOFR was intended for the purpose of medical research. No doubt GOFR may have medical research benefits but what about any nefarious attempts to use it to develop a weapon? It is no secret that China has held to such ambitions. A research group known as "Defense One" that provides technical analysis and intelligence on U.S. defense and national security published an interesting article on August 14, 2019, just months prior to the SARS-CoV-2 outbreak in China, about the push for the Chinese

---

[106] Fox News, November 4, 2021, *Rand Paul Accuses Fauci of Changing 'Gain-of-Function' Definition*, site accessed on December 16, 2021 from https://www.foxnews.com/politics/rand-paul-anthony-fauci-senate-hearing-gain-of-function.

[107] Andrew Mark Miller, *Fox News Special Report Outlines Fresh Questions on What Fauci, Government Knew About COVID Origin*, January 26, 2022. https://www.foxnews.com/politics/special-report-outlines-fresh-questions-on-what-fauci-government-knew-about-covid-origin.

military to develop gene editing. The article mentioned this research as a goal of the military to attain tactical superiority: "In 2010's *War for Biological Dominance,* Guo Jiwei, a professor with the Third Military Medical University, emphasizes the impact of biology on future warfare and how biology is considered among the seven new domains of warfare with an offensive capability."[108] Kennedy further describes the ongoing funding and strange collaboration between U.S. GOFR and Wuhan: "the escalating intramural arms race to capture Pentagon, CIA, BARDA, DARPA, and HHS biosecurity funding was pulling the military, CIA, and NIAID deeper and deeper into the dicey alchemy of 'gain-of-function research' that would ultimately culminate inside the BSL-4 Pandora's box in Wuhan."[109]

From Bats to Bioweapons

---

[108] Elsa B. Kania & Wilson Vorndick, August 14, 2019, *Weaponizing Biotech: How China's Military is Preparing for a New Domain of Warfare.* Source accessed on October 25, 2021 from https://www.defenseone.com/ideas//2019/08/chinas-military-pursuing-biotech/159167/

[109] Kennedy, *The Real Anthony Fauci*, 820.

China's risky research with the viral pathogens from bats starts with an incident in an abandoned copper mineshaft in the Yunnan province.[110] In April 2012 there were six miners who were given the task of cleaning out all the bat fecal matter that had accumulated in the mineshaft. However, by the end of the month all the miners became ill with a severe respiratory pneumonia with fever, cough, and shortness of breath and three of them died. In the Wuhan WIV the surviving miners tested positive for SARS antibodies and a strange SARS-like virus. The chief scientist in Wuhan who became engaged with the research following this incident is none other than Dr. Shi Zhengli who is a subject matter expert in zoonotic diseases in bat populations. In 2015 Zhengli coauthored an important research paper with Ralph Baric at UNC title *A SARS-Like Cluster of Circulating Bat Coronaviruses Shows Potential for Human Emergence* which stated:

Using the SARS-CoV reverse genetics system, we generated and characterized a chimeric virus expressing the spike of bat coronavirus SHC014 in a mouse-adapted SARS-CoV backbone...On the basis of these findings, we synthetically, re-derived an infectious full-length SHC014 recombinant virus and demonstrate robust viral replication both *in vitro* and *in vivio*. Our work suggests a potential risk of SARS-CoV re-emergence from viruses currently circulating in bat populations.[111]

The paper underscores the GOFR projects being done collaboratively with Wuhan and UNC as it highlights "reverse genetic systems generated from a chimeric virus" related to SARS-CoV-2. After the incident with the illness that the miners had succumbed to, Markson reported that Zhengli's team visited the caves four times over eleven months collecting samples in which "they identified 150

---

[110] Markson, *What Really Happened in Wuhan*, 245-247.

[111] Nature Medicine: Vol. 21, No. 12, December 2015, *A SARS-Like Cluster of Circulating Bat Coronaviruses Shows Potential for Human Emergence*, Nature America Inc.

alphacoronaviruses and two betacoronaviruses – and one of these was a SARS-like betacoronarirus."[112]

A scientific paper that was published in October 2020 focused on the links between the illnesses of the miners and SARS-CoV-2. The paper was actually adapted from a Master's Thesis from a WIV researcher before being removed from the Chinese websites and concluded "that a SARS-like CoV originating from Chinese horseshoe bats (*Rhinolophus*) was the predicted causative agent."[113] The paper's thesis proposed that the mineshaft pathogen could provide important clues to the origins of SARS-CoV-2. What is significant about this research publication is that it could reveal a "smoking gun" hypothesis that SARS-CoV-2 had links to the research on this virus in the Wuhan lab: "The same virus 4991 was renamed as RaTG13, which is the next genetic relative of SARS-CoV-2" and raises serious questions. First, why would such significant information not be made available during the initial pandemic and secondly why were the miner's illnesses not reported to the WHO? Also why did programs like PREDICT not mention this lethal pneumonia? The paper also brings up the fact that there must have been underlying reasons for the WIV research team to continue visiting the mines until October 2014 without any further public disclosure. An MIT Pandemic Technology Project published on June 2021 by Rowan Jacobsen addresses the risky research that was undertaken by Baric and Zhengli when they detected the genome of the new virus referred to as SHC014 relative to the original SARS virus: "Baric had developed a way around that problem – a technique for "reverse genetics in coronaviruses. Not only did it allow him to bring an actual virus to life from its genetic code, but he could mix and match parts of multiple viruses...The resulting chimera would demonstrate

---

[112] Markson, *What Really Happened in Wuhan*, 247.

[113] Monali C. Rahalkar and Rahul A. Bahulikar, *Letha Pneumonia Cases in Mojiang Miners (2012) and the Mineshaft Could Provide Important Clues to the Origin of SARS-CoV-2*, Frontiers in Public Health, October 20, 2020. Vol. 8; Article 581569.

whether the spike of SHC014 would attach to human cells."[114] The MIT project further reveals the GOFR work collaborated between UNC and Wuhan with the "introduction of a virus modified with that code into mice and into a petri dish of human airway cells" demonstrating that this Coronavirus could easily transmit to humans. With the scope of project focus into the feasibility of human transmission of the virus, the potential for a pandemic is highly likely. The *Science Daily* quoted Baric on the human spread potential of the virus to create a pandemic: "So, this is not a situation of 'if there will be an outbreak of one of those coronaviruses but rather when and how prepared we'll be to address it."[115] The article continues: "Baric and his team demonstrated that the newly-identified SARS-like virus, labeled SHC014-CoV and found in the Chinese horseshoe bats, can jump between bats and humans by showing that the virus can latch onto and use the same human and bat receptor for entry. The virus also replicates as well as SARS-CoV in primary human lung cells."

The GOFR researchers were aware of the potential of the coronaviruses they were working with in collaboration with Wuhan for starting a deadly pandemic. Not only had they discovered that the SARS-CoV could easily infect humans, but they also found that the virus had the capability for transmission as it could easily replicate in human lung cells. A research abstract published by Dr. Carlos Farkas noted the unique structure of the virus which enhanced its ability to rapidly spread: "One of the striking genomic features of this novel virus is the presence of a novel furin-like cleavage site in the S-protein of the virus, which differs from SARS-CoV-1 and may have implications for the life

---

[114] Rowan Jacobsen, *Inside the Risky Bat-Virus Engineering that Links America to Wuhan*, June 29, 2021, MIT Pandemic Technology Project. Source accessed October 15, 2021, from https://www.technologyreview.com/2021/06/29/1027290/gain-of-function-risky-bat-virus-engineering- links-america-to-wuhan/

[115] *Science Daily*, November 10, 2015, University of North Carolina at Chapel Hill. Site accessed July 6, 2021 from https://www.sciencedaily.com/releases/2015/11/151110115711.htm

cycle and pathogenicity of the novel virus."[116] What is significant about this finding of the "novel furin-like cleavage site in the S-protein" is that it demonstrates that aside from natural mutation, the virus could have been developed through artificial means being directly manipulated in a lab environment. Dr. Farkas also refers to RaTG13 bat-derived coronavirus as having as much as 88% identity to SARS-CoV-2. This provides another direct link to the miner's outbreak in China and the same virus attributed to the pandemic as stated in the research abstract: "As a proof of concept, in the early beginning of the outbreak in China, sequencing the virus from nine patients from Wuhan in China revealed 99.9% similarity among samples. That finding suggests 2019-nCoV originated from one source within a very short time, supporting the clonality of spreading." The virus samples that Zhengli was working with in the Wuhan lab have a close connection to the pandemic SARS-CoV-2. This type of tracing of genomic viral origins is what is referred to as "bioinformatics" and is a scientific process within epidemiological investigative study that is now beginning to emerge which provides evidence that the source of the virus originated in the Wuhan lab and not from naturally occurring zoonotic sources. Other bioinformatic researchers such as Dr. Liji Thomas have observed the unique characteristics of the viruses spike gene in which there is low probability for a naturally occurring origin especially considering the RaTG13 that was isolated in 2013: "This insertion could have occurred by random insertion mutation, recombination or by laboratory insertion. The researchers say the possibility of random insertion is too low to explain the origin of this motif."[117] These unique viral properties

---

[116] Carlos Farkas, Abstract: *Insights on Early Mutational Events in SARS-CoV-2 Virus Reveal Founder Effects Across Geographical Regions*, May 21, 2020. Source accessed on June 24, 2021 from https://peerj.com/articles/articles/9255/#supplementary-material

[117] Liji Thomas, *The Origin of SARS-CoV-2 Furin Cleavage Site Remains a Mystery*. News Medical Life Sciences, February 17, 2021. Source accessed December 20, 2021 from https://www.news-medical.net/news/20210217 /The-origin-of-SARS-CoV-2-furin-cleavage-site-remains-a-mystery.aspx

within SARS-CoV-2 such as the links within the RaTG13 and the furin cleavage site within the spike proteins are indicative of a laboratory origin rather than a naturally occurring biological source. In addition to the viral samples taken from the 2012 miner's outbreak, there is further evidence that demonstrates direct genetic manipulation of the virus to unleash a pandemic. Further investigative research into the RNA sequencing data of the early COVID-19 patient samples provide us with some fascinating insights.

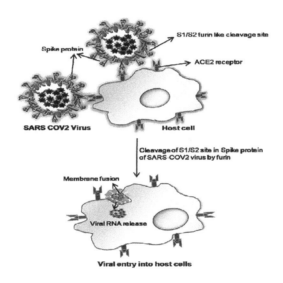

Evidence of Cross-Contamination of Viral Samples

In Chapter 7 we will talk more about the courageous scientists and researchers who are challenging the popular media narrative that is being promoted about the pandemic's natural origins. These brave individuals put their professional careers and personal reputation at risk to stand up to those on the left who are tolerant of China's oppressive military regime. To even mention a lab origin possibility (whether it is an intentional or accidental lab leak hypothesis) is condemned as being "anti-science" or a "conspiracy theorist" by the mainline media and the progressive elites. One such scientist who is bravely leading the way investigating the truth behind the Wuhan incident is Dr. Steven C. Quay.

Dr. Quay is an accomplished cancer research physician and is CEO for clinical-stage therapeutics company. He has taken an active role in his investigational research into the Wuhan lab. One of Dr. Quay's research projects was undertaken along with several other prominent subject matter experts in bioinformatics. In this work he looks at the RNA sequencing data of early COVID-19 patient samples: "The Wuhan Institute of Virology published a description of five early patients with COVID-19 that has been one of the most cited papers from the early days of the pandemic. Previous reports have examined the raw SRA files from this WIV paper and have identified significant anomalous sequence data...A contamination signature of three sequences is present in similar proportions in all WIV specimens, suggesting at least in part, a shared contamination process or step."[118] According to Dr. Quay this raised a "red flag" as it revealed that these samples contained the presence of an influenza vaccine specifically for H7N9. Other questions are raised in the research paper: "How did the H7N9 enter the humans when there are no records of trials of any oral or nasal vaccines being used at that time in Wuhan?" Another possibility that is considered is whether the infections were caused by some lab material, or a lab worker being infected with a mouse being used in an experiment? Dr. Quay points to the GOFR projects that were being done in the Wuhan lab as source of the infection: "It is well known that WIV was working with SARS-like coronaviruses and used humanized mice, i.e., hACE-2 expressing mice. So, could cross-contamination of the mice with H7N9 and SARS-CoV-2 be a possibility, looking at the co-occurrence of these sequences?"

---

[118] Steven C. Quay, Monali C. Rahalkar, Adrian Jones, and Rahul Bahulikar, *Contamination or Vaccine Research? RNA Sequencing of Early COVID-19 Patient Samples Show Abnormal Presence of Vectorized H7N9 Hemagglutinin Segment* (2021).

-1 reading frame insertion　　　　　　　　**FCS**

SARS-CoV-2　671　C A S Y Q T Q T N S P R R A R S V A S Q S I I A　694
23573　ucg gcu agu uau cag acu cag acu uc**U** C**C**U C**C**G C**C**G **G**Ca cgu agu gua gcu agu caa ucc auc auugcc　23644

BtCoV RaTG13　23555　ucg gcc agu uau cag acu cag acu uc- - - - - - - - - - -acgu agu gua gcu agu aucu acu auugcc　23614
671　C A S Y Q T Q T N S　　　　　　R S V A S Q S I I A　690

-2 reading frame insertion　　　　　　　　**FCS**

SARS-CoV-2　671　C A S Y Q T Q T N S P R R A R S V A S Q S I I A　694
23573　ucg gcu agu uau cag acu cag acu uc**U** C**C**U C**C**G C**C**G **G**Ca cgu agu gua gcu agu caa ucc auc auugcc　23644

BtCoV RaTG13　23555　ucg gcc agu uau cag acu cag acu aau u- - - - - - - - -ca cgu agu gtg gcc agu caa ucu auu auugcc　23614
671　C A S Y Q T Q T N S　　　　　　R S V A S Q S I I A　690

B　　　　　　　**Betacoronavirus Subgenera**

Sarbeco	SARS-CoV-2	671	CASYQTQTNS--PRRARSVASQSIIA	694
	BtCoV RmYN02	631	CASY----NS--P-AAR-VGTNSIIA	647
	BtCoV RaTG13	671	CASYQTQTNS------RSVASQSIIA	690
	SARS-CoV	657	CASYHTVSLL------RSTSQKSIVA	676
Merbeco	MERS-CoV	736	CALPDTPST-LTPRSVRSVPGEMRLA	760
	BtCoV HKU5	739	CAIPPTTSS----RFRRATSGVPDVF	760
	BtCoV HKU4	740	CAVPPVSTF-------RSYSASQ--F	756
Embeco	HCoV HKU1a	744	CVDYNSPSSSSSRRKRRSISASYRFV	769
	HCoV HKU1b	743	CIDYALPS---SRRKRRGISSPYRFV	765
	HCoV OC43	756	CLDYSK-----NRRSRRAILTGYRFT	776
	Bovine CoV	757	CVDYST-----KRRSRRSITTGYRFT	775
	RatCoV HKU24	752	CVDYSS-----TWRAKRDLNTGYRLT	770
Hibeco	BtCov HpZj13	714	CVNYTAD---TRLRTARAADRALTFN	736
	BtCov HcNG08	698	CLNITRG-----RVGSRSAGHLKESS	718

Optimal FCS **RXR/KR** or **RRXR/KR**; minimal FCS **RXXR**

Monobasic cleavage site **R**; predicted O-linked glycan **S/T**

This assumption lines up with what we previously mentioned that Zhengli with Wuhan Lab and Baric from UNC were working on a specific GOFR project as early as 2015 for the introduction of a virus modified with a code into mice and into a petri dish of human airway cells. It is also reported that Zhengli was trained on this procedure by American research scientists at UNC and possibly Baric himself.[119] Furthermore, it was discovered that there were other contaminant viruses in lower proportions including Nipah which should warrant grave concerns for the development of a bioweapon. Although Nipah virus can be introduced naturally from zoonotic sources such as bats and swine it is classified as a Category C biological agent. This is because Nipah like SARS-CoV-2 (which also has a Category C classification) is an extremely lethal pathogen that can be engineered as a bioweapon to create a pandemic. Nipah is even considered much more deadly than SARS-CoV-2. Dr. Quay's research raises serious concerns

---

[119] Markson, *What Really Happened in Wuhan*, 201.

regarding the intent and purposes behind the lab research conducted in Wuhan. Were the GOFR projects seeking to develop deadly viral strains for nefarious purposes and included vaccine development research in the perspective of potential viral pathogen antidotes? If it was it a lab accident, did a Wuhan lab worker become infected during GOFR projects or did an environmental lab breach result in a release into the local population (lab leak theory)?

The investigative report presented to the House of Foreign Affairs provides additional details on the WIV's work on bat coronaviruses. According to the report, Zhengli also began working with Peter Daszak the CEO of EcoHealth Alliance in 2004 to conduct research to determine the origins of the 2002 SARS pandemic.[120] Funding for this research was provided to EcoHealth Alliance through grants (Federal Grant Numbers 2005CB523004 and 2005AA219070) from the Department of Health and Human Services (HHS), National Institutes of Health (NIH), National Science Foundation (NSF), and the United States Agency for International Development (USAID). Including EcoHealth AllinanceThese are the "big five" agencies through which taxpayers funded GOFR projects in Wuhan. For nearly sixteen years Zhengli and Daszak collaborated on coronavirus research during the same time frame that expedition teams were gathering bat fecal samples from the mines where the outbreak occurred and other bat caves. Also at a 2016 conference, Daszak mentioned his research projects with Wuhan: "My colleagues in China did the work. You create pseudoparticles, you insert the spike proteins from those viruses, see if they bind to human cells. At each step of this you move closer and closer to this virus that could really become pathogenic in people."[121] Numerous collaborative research articles were published to include *Isolation and Characterization of a Novel Bat Coronavirus Closely Related to the Direct Progenitor of Severe Acute Respiratory Syndrome Coronavirus.*

---

[120] *The Origins of COVID-19: An Investigation of the Wuhan Institute of Virology;* Evidence of Genetic Modification, 30.

[121] Markson, *What Really Happened in Wuhan*, 182-183.

This article states: "the WIV reported the successful isolation of second novel coronavirus, WIV16. The SARS-like coronavirus was isolated from a single sample of bat fecal matter collected in Kunming, Yunnan Province of the PRC in July 2013." The next paper which followed this study included details on a "SARS-like WIV1-CoV poised for human emergence" (the WIV1 designation is a reference to the source lab: Wuhan Institute of Virology – WIV). It is within this context that the GOFR project began creating the chimeric (artificial) viruses to study their capability for producing global pandemics. As previously mentioned GOFR directly modified these viral strains from the bat fecal samples using processes involving reverse genetic systems which also created eight separate chimeric viruses by inserting the spike proteins of various SARS-like coronaviruses. These viral pathogens created in Wuhan through joint funding with NIAID and USAID's PREDICT program had the capacity to infect humans even before their BSL-4 lab was fully operational.

In 2018 the Chinese Academy of Science launched a project titled *Pathogen Host Adaption and Immune Intervention* where Zhengli was appointed as research lead. This project focused upon the "traceability and evolution of new viral pathogens" as well as their ability to transmit to human populations.[122] Also in the same year she was appointed principal investigator for a new "Strategic Priority Research Program" that focused upon the "genetic evolution and transmission mechanism of bat-borne viruses' with $1.35 million in funding. Another grant project of $850,000 was provided to run through December 2021 that specialized in "replication and modification of coronaviruses." The GOFR projects that were funded included experiments testing chimeric coronaviruses in 2018 and 2019. According to Daszak the goal of the research was to "insert some of these other related [viruses] and get a better vaccine." The research experimentation was about genetically manipulating coronaviruses and testing

---

[122] *The Origins of COVID-19: An Investigation of the Wuhan Institute of Virology.* Evidence of Genetic Modification, 35.

them against human immune systems in 2018 and 2019 prior to the pandemic. This no doubt led to the engineering of a modified virus with the enhanced ability for SARS-CoV-2's spike protein to bind with human ACE2. Dr. Baric and his team using a "novel genetic engineering system for SARS-CoV genomes" at UNC described the SARS-CoV DNA as having stealth-like properties with a "no-see-um" characteristic. In other words, the ability to trace the virus from a zoonotic origin that is naturally occurring from animal species from that which is genetically engineered in a lab would not be readily apparent. Baric adds another detail about this specific GOFR work, "Molecularly cloned viruses were indistinguishable from wild type."

Research Supporting a Lab Origins Hypothesis

There is considerable evidence which points to a laboratory origin of SARS-CoV-2 in what we have covered in the collaborative GOFR research conducted between NIH and its principal agency partners (HHS, USAID, EcoHealth, etc.) and the Wuhan lab. A research work that puts "the icing on the cake" for a lab origins hypothesis comes with Dr. Quay's comprehensive 193-page data analysis that was published on January 29, 2021, with this thesis: "A Bayesian analysis concludes beyond a reasonable doubt that SARS-CoV-2 is not a natural zoonosis but instead is laboratory derived."[123] This very important research examines WIV's analysis of bronchial lavage specimens from ICU patients at the Wuhan Jinyintan Hospital in December 2019 with the use of a Bayes Theorem analysis to evaluate both the zoonotic (naturally occurring) origin hypothesis and a laboratory (synthetically derived) origin hypothesis. While the focus of Quay's paper is not on a Bio-Weapon hypothesis, he does initially address it in his introduction: "But was SARS-Co-2 more than just a gain-of-function experiment that escaped a laboratory? Could it have been one part of a two-part

---

[123] Steven C. Quay, MD, PhD, *Bayesian Analysis of SARS-CoV-2 Origin*, January 29, 2021, Steven@DrQuay.com.

novel virus-vaccine bioweapons program?" While he admits the possibility of a bioweapon's intent, Quay also calls for the need to gather further data: "It is also urgent to gather further data to support or refute if this was a Chinese bioweapons program, as the consequences of that would be significant." Quay focuses his research on the consideration of only two hypothesis – a zoonotic origin or a laboratory origin rather than to include a bioweapons hypothesis. This is due to the fact that he chose to deal with the greater volume of documentary research that was readily available: "In the absence of any such documentary evidence that bioweapon research was being conducted or that SARS-CoV-2 is a bioweapon and to take the least inflammatory posture, the initial state for the above prior analysis will be recalculated by eliminating the hypothesis, and its accompanying probability, that SARS-CoV-2 was created as a bioweapon." Also since his work is a comparative approach to popular mainline arguments set forth in support of a zoonotic origin arguments endorsed by Daszak along with EcoHealth and NIH against the lab origins arguments, Quay devotes his focus solely on these two hypotheses excluding a bioweapons intent all together. The research presented is quite careful to not draw inferences from conjectures that lack specific evidence. He states: "There is no direct evidence of whether the release was accidental, or deliberate but circumstantial evidence makes it highly likely it was accidental." In fact, his initial assessment only lends a 3% probability for a bioweapons hypothesis which is quite low in his assessment. After a thorough and objective analysis of the zoonotic origin hypothesis and the laboratory origin hypothesis, Quay concludes that a laboratory origin is the most likely explanation with a 99.5% confidence rating.

Could the Lab Origin Findings Provide
Reasonable Support for a Bioweapons Hypothesis?

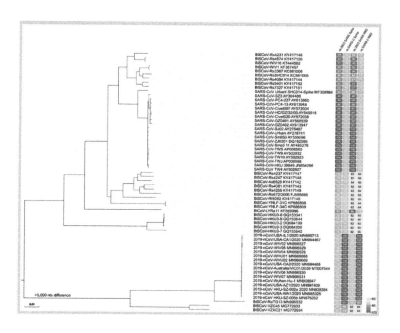

I have tremendous respect and appreciation for Dr. Quay's research which defends his central thesis that SARS-CoV-2 had its origin in the Wuhan lab. The pandemic did not originate with a naturally occurring pathogen; rather it was deliberately engineered in a laboratory environment. To remain objective and unbiased in his research, he does not speculate on the intent of the Chinese or discuss what motives they had in their GOFR project which unleashed one of the deadliest global pathogens in pandemic history. Therefore, his thesis focuses upon the likelihood of an accidental lab leak. This is a reasonable assumption given the fact that the Wuhan lab was known to be environmentally unsafe, and they did not always adhere to standard BSL-4 protocols while working with these dangerous pathogens. Some of the prior research was even conducted before their BSL-4 lab was completely operational. Even the slightest error within any GOFR projects would easily prove to be catastrophic. The possibility for human error in any laboratory environment cannot be ruled out. It is not a question of whether a lab accident will happen or not, but it is rather a question of when it will happen. When such an accident occurs BSL-4 standards require specific protocols for containment and protection for their personnel and especially for the safety of the community in which the lab is located. Lab staff must be thoroughly trained and equipped with the proper level of personal protective equipment (PPE). In my past work in bioterrorism preparedness our program directly funded a BSL-3 lab that was part of the national lab response network for emerging pathogens and category A agents. I was trained and certified in the use of level 4 PPE to include PAPR (powered air purifying respirators) equipment and personally conducted training and fit testing of personnel not only for biological PPE but also chemical and radiological PPE. Lab safety training and adequate PPE are essential for such work. However, it has been reported that the Wuhan lab staff only utilized basic N95 respirators and sometimes did not wear the full level 4 gear to include boots, hood, and gloves.[124] Given these factors with the inadequate levels of preparedness capabilities of the Wuhan lab staff and facilities, the chances for a lab accident were quite high.

I do not rule out the possibility for a lab accident or an accidental breach in containment that could have released SARS-CoV-2 into the local population creating a global pandemic. However, I believe that it is important that we also consider what the purpose and the possible intent for China to create such a deadly pathogen whether the release was accidental or intentional. Some would insist that China was developing the virus for medical and humanitarian purposes such as for vaccine research. Nevertheless, considering the extraordinary efforts behind China's cover-up (censorship, silencing of local citizens, etc.) and lack of transparency when the virus first became public makes

---

[124] Markson, *What Really Happened in Wuhan*, 175.

this highly suspicious. Why would the Chinese government go to such efforts for hiding what happened? Some even say that China was too embarrassed to admit the outbreak had happened due to the pride taken with their public image. This is a weak excuse given that the CCP state media began to build the wet market origins source immediately refusing to allow any assistance from other countries to help investigate the virus. While we may never have complete proof of what the intent or motive of the CCP in their GOFR projects, it is important that our national security and defense not to completely dismiss the possibility that China created the virus for nefarious purposes. While a bioweapons hypothesis is largely speculative since we do not have absolute proof to substantiate such a claim, I would like to summarize some circumstantial evidence which could provide support that SARS-CoV-2 was developed as a weapon of mass destruction:

1. The Chinese military and more specifically the People's Liberation Army (PLA) has been directly involved with the WIV. PLA Major General Chen Wei an expert in biological and chemical weapons was assigned to the WIV. Although the official CCP media statement regarding Wei's appointment was released in January 2020, it is likely that she was involved with the WIV as early as 2017 because of her high-profile position. Wei is a chief researcher at the Academy of Military Medical Sciences in Beijing and member of the Chinese People's Political Consultative Conference (CPPCC) among the highest level of decision-making authority. Other high-level scientists and WIV staff are closely affiliated with the Communist party and their State Media.

2. China has a long-standing interest in the research and development of biological weapons of mass destruction since the early days of Mao's communist revolution. Col. Liang and Col. Xiangsui of the PLA have documented their ambitions to create

viral pathogens capable of creating global pandemics with the purpose of defeating their enemies "without firing a shot".

3. Communist China is a ruthless military regime with an army of over 2 million active-duty personnel bent on world conquest. The release of a bioweapon causing a pandemic would help them gain advantage as a world power especially when global economies are adversely impacted. The pandemic has not slowed down the rapid pace of their military advance with the building of artificial islands for military bases and the development of their long-range supersonic missile systems capable of deploying nuclear warheads.

4. China's bioengineered viral pathogens are classified as Category C agents capable of producing pandemics. The presence of Nipah virus in the specimens from Wuhan demonstrate their concerted effort to enhance biological pathogens making them highly infectious and easily transmissible to local populations.

5. China's military conducted large scale pandemic response training exercises in Wuhan in September 2019 just prior to the Military World Games in October. These exercises included both military and medical personnel to enhance their preparedness capabilities for epidemiological contact tracing, isolation and quarantine procedures and medical countermeasures.

6. The Military World Games held in October 2019 in Wuhan may have been the initial deployment of SARS-CoV-2 to enable the rapid infection and spread of the virus through the world's military personnel. Many of the military personnel became ill with SARS like symptoms shortly after they returned to their home countries.

7.   Before the Military games the WIV's viral database of more than 22,000 samples collected from bats and mice was suddenly taken offline between 2:00am and 3:00am on September 12, 2019. The immediate area around Wuhan's lab also went into black-out in an apparent effort to hide activity from the public.

8.   Two members of Zhengli's research editorial board were linked to the U.S. Army's biological lab in Fort Detrick, Maryland (USAMRIID). This is alarming to find that Wuhan had access to a top-secret military biological weapons lab given that China has been guilty of intellectual property theft on past occasions at various U.S. research institutions. When the Fort Detrick lab was working with Gilead Sciences in developing a treatment for Ebola known as Remdesivir, a patent for the medication was immediately filed in China by the WIV. This patent filing in Wuhan is highly suspicious. Although now proven not to be as effective as some of the readily available "repurposed medications" Remdesivir is standardly prescribed for COVID-19. This collaboration was allowed even when U.S. intelligence had proven that the WIV had ties directly to the Chinese military.[125] Could the research theft been motivated by China's quest for a COVID-19 antiviral when Wuhan was developing a bioweapon or could big pharma and the PLA have shared involvement with Wuhan for the creation of Remdesivir?

9.   In July 2019 Canada's only BSL-4 lab had an incident with the dismissal of Chinese virologist Qiu Xiangguo who was caught sending deadly viral samples to the Wuhan lab. Ebola and Nipah were also sent from this lab to China at the requests of the WIV.

---

[125] Markson, *What Really Happened in Wuhan*, 226.

10. Sheri Markson's investigative team makes an excellent observation: "China's People's Liberation Army has been involved in scientific research into the origins of Coronavirus." According to Markson a study published on March 26, 2020, focused on how SARS-CoV-2 transferred from animals to humans. The study utilized data from a microbiology lab in the Liberation Army's Academy of Medical Sciences to conduct its genetic sequencing and viral isolation. The Director of the PLA microbiology institute Colonel Cao Wuchan is acknowledged in the study.[126]

11. Mike Pompeo who served as CIA Director from 2017 to 2018 and later as the U.S. Secretary of State in the Trump Administration assembled a team to provide a research dossier on activities in Wuhan. The team included National Security Advisor Robert O'Brien and Miles Yu, Principal Chinese Policy Planning Advisor. The team focused on the nefarious intent of Communist China and concluded with their suspicion regarding the possibility of a genetically engineered bioweapon by utilizing SARS-CoV-2. Intelligence that was declassified in January 2021 tells of "secret military activity at the WIV" and that it has been actively engaged with military research projects since 2017.

12. A book by the title of *The Unnatural Origin of SARS and New Species of Man-Made Viruses as Genetic Bioweapons* was written in 2015 by top Chinese military scientists stated that coronaviruses could be "artificially manipulated into an emerging human disease virus, then weaponized and unleashed in a way never seen before." The book further adds "these engineered viruses will lead to a new era of genetic weapons."[127]

---

[126] Ibid, 264.

[127] Javin Aryan, *A Look at China's Biowarfare Ambitions*, June 2, 2021, Observer Research Foundation. Source Accessed January 4, 2022 from https://www.orfonline.org/expert-speak/a-look-at-chinas-biowarfare-ambitions/

13. The WIV also houses the Wuhan Institute of Biological Products (WIBP) which has been involved with the development of COVID vaccines. It has been suspected that the WIBP is directly involved in a bioweapons program. The vaccine research initially ended in 2008 but resumed in 2017 working with SARS and MERS by using genetically engineered viruses. The vaccine research was funded by the Chinese as a key biopharmaceutical project.

This lists some of the circumstantial evidence that could provide support for the hypothesis that SARS-CoV-2 was developed by Communist China with the intent and purpose to release a bioweapon. Whether this may have happened prematurely by accidental release or was part of the plan for an intentional deployment at the World Military Games remains a mystery. The motives and intent of China for its GOFR projects that engineered enhanced viral pathogens may never fully come to light. However, the fact remains that this virus was intentionally developed in the Wuhan lab through genetic engineering. We will now turn to the aftermath of Wuhan's GOFR project with the continued lies and deceit of the agency directors collaborating with the WIV.

CHAPTER 5

IN THE AFTERMATH OF WUHAN: DECEIT, PROPAGANDA & CONTROL

The Chinese Communist Party's culpability in deliberately covering up the virus instead of alerting the world is a crime as shameful and abhorrent as the Tiananmen Square massacre. Millions of lives have been lost, and counting, with families in every corner of the earth struck by tragedy, while economies have been decimated, livelihoods lost, and people thrown into poverty. – Sharri Markson, Investigative Journalist

An Investigation Launched by The Pompeo Team

Mike Pompeo served as CIA Director from 2017 to 2018 and later was appointed as Secretary of State in the Trump Administration. Pompeo was keenly aware of the threat that Communist China represented not only to U.S. security and defense but also to the international community at large. He called for full accountability for the Tiananmen Square victims on the massacre's 30th anniversary.[128] Pompeo had also been an outspoken critic of globalist policies that undermined American national sovereignty and the

---

[128] Nahal Toosi, *Pompeo Blasts China on Anniversary of Tiananmen Square Massacre*, June 3, 2019, Politico. Source accessed January 4, 2022 from https://www.politico. eu/article/pompeo-china-tiananmen-square-massacre/

trend in pandering to China in previous administrations. In a speech to the Hudson Institute in October 2019, Pompeo made the following remarks about China's threat: "Today, we're finally realizing the degree to which the Chinese Communist Party is truly hostile to the United States and our values...We know too that the Chinese Communist Party is offering its people and the world an entirely different model of governance. It's one in which a Leninist Party rules, and everyone must think and act according to the will of the Communist elites." [129] In the early onset of the pandemic, he had suspicions of China as they were in the very epicenter of the outbreak and the fact that there was a total lack of transparency in disclosing specific information about the rapidly escalating pathogen. He wondered if any nefarious motives for the virus might be the reasons for a cover up by China. Pompeo soon committed himself to the task of developing an investigation team that would inquire into the origins of the virus and to gather any intelligence that might be helpful in determining what contributed to lack of containment and how the Wuhan outbreak so quickly went out of control. The investigation team included National Security Advisor Robert O'Brien and State Department China Policy Planning Advisor Miles Yu. Yu was assigned the responsibility of putting together a dossier on China's handling of the virus to include their research lab in Wuhan, the Chinese Military, and the role of the CCP. O'Brien stated that "The Chinese are going to use this virus that they allowed to spread around the world to increase their power and dominion."[130] Yu's dossier also contains an interesting note that China had been working on a COVID-19 vaccine prior to the pandemic: "It may seem likely that WIV has been researching a vaccine before the outbreak."[131] This comes within the context of the development of Remdesivir when

---

[129] Michael R. Pompeo at the Hudson Institute's Herman Kahn Award Gala, October 30, 2019. Site accessed January 13, 2022 from https://uy.usembassy.gov/michael-r-pompeo-at-the-hudson-institutes-herman-kahn-award-gala/

[130] Markson, *What Really Happened in Wuhan*, 121.

[131] Ibid.

Fauci sent samples of the medication to China and immediately the WIV filed a commercial patent for the drug. Yu's dossier also addresses China's bioweapon research and Shi Zhengli's genetically engineered viruses and went on to say how it was quite feasible for COVID to have been made in the Wuhan lab. The investigation was also focused on any possibility that the CCP planned to use the virus to gain any political or military superiority in its global affairs.

The findings of this investigation by the team were released by Trump in April 2020 and the following month Pompeo emphasized again that the possibility that COVID was created in a lab. The next step called for a formal commission to research the origins of the virus with the stated purpose:

The Commission shall investigate the origins of the Covid-19 pandemic; the economic, political, social, human, and other costs of the pandemic borne by the United States; and whether the People's Republic of China or the Chinese Communist Party have used the pandemic to advance their own economic, geopolitical, military, or territorial agendas. [132]

---

[132] Markson, *What Really Happened in Wuhan*, 150.

The executive order to activate the commission was set to be signed but it was stalled out and "dead-on-arrival." As soon as the preliminary reports were released to the public an immediate firestorm of hostile criticism came from mainline media saying that it was nothing more than a conspiracy theory. This came as no surprise since the political atmosphere in Washington had been already charged with calls for Trump's impeachment and accusations of Russian collusion in the previous years. By this time media cynics saw Pompeo's investigation on the virus lab origins as an opportunity to further target the Trump administration and to undermine any public credibility in the investigation.

The "Scarlet Letter" of Anti-Science Accusations

The mainstream media overwhelmingly were supportive of the narrative spun by the CDC, NIH, WHO, and Wuhan that SARS-CoV-2 had a naturally occurring zoonotic origin. Along with the increasing media hostility against a lab origins theory, authorities within most of the scientific community also aligned themselves with Wuhan by criticizing dissenting views as "anti-science." Dr. Zhengli in response to an inquiry that the virus originated in her Wuhan lab was quick to defend herself: "Those who believe and spread rumors, shut your dirty mouth."[133] Very few scientific researchers were willing to risk their funding by daring to challenge the mainstream narrative. The NIH, CDC and the HHS were the "gate-keepers" to billions of dollars in research grants and they were not hesitant to wield their influence over those who published their research in prominent medical and scientific journals. The highly esteemed international medical journal, *The Lancet* was also quick to defend a SARS-CoV-2 zoonotic theory and to deny a lab origins theory with a public letter signed by twenty-seven prominent scientists by claiming that the lab theory was only spreading misinformation: "Conspiracy theories do nothing

---

[133] Ibid, 191.

but create fear, rumors, and prejudice that jeopardize our global collaboration in the fight against the virus. We support the call from the Director-General of WHO to promote scientific evidence and unity over misinformation and conjecture."[134] It is not surprising that one of the primary authors and signers of the Lancet letter is none other than Peter Daszak the CEO of EcoHealth Alliance that are co-collaborators of the GOFR with NIH and Wuhan. The statement is in solidarity with the WHO and Daszak was one of the few Americans permitted on the WHO investigation team allowed to have access into the Wuhan Lab.

It is simply amazing that Daszak's admission on the WHO team was not challenged as a conflict of interest considering his ties to Wuhan. The WHO team came away from Wuhan with glowing reports of how cooperative the WIV was and that they found nothing indicative of a lab breach. Yet, they did not provide any solid evidence to the scientific community to support their claims. Markson further adds the impact that the Lancet statement had on the international scientific community: "The *Lancet* letter was extremely effective. From that moment forward, anyone who dared suggest a non-natural origin of the virus was labeled a conspiracy theorist in the media. It worked to dissuade other reputable scientists from speaking out."[135] Fauci in sync with the Lancet letter issued a public statement on behalf of the CDC and NIH in support of the zoonotic origin theory that it came from bats. Daszak promptly sent Fauci an email personally thanking him for his statement: "I just wanted to say a personal thank you on behalf of our staff and collaborators, for publicly standing up and stating that the scientific evidence supports a natural origin for Covid-19 from a bat-to-human spillover, not a lab release from the Wuhan Institute

---

[134] The Lancet, *Statement in Support of the Scientists, Public Health Professionals, and Medical Professionals of China Combatting COVID-19.* Volume 395; Issue 10226, E42-E43, March, 07, 2020. Source accessed January 18, 2022 from https://www.thelancet.com/journals/lancet/article / PIIS0140-6736(20)30418-9/fulltext.

[135] Markson, *What Really Happened in Wuhan*, 271.

of Virology...From my perspective, your comments are brave, and coming from your trusted voice, will help dispel the myths being spun around the virus' origin."[136] Daszak realized the strategic advantage in having Fauci "America's Doctor" the voice highly respected by the mainstream media to also release public statements in support of the natural origins theory of the virus. The full circle of collaboration becomes apparent between EcoHealth Alliance, CDC, NIH and Wuhan as the purveyors of media propaganda especially if they can shift public attention away from their involvement with their GOFR projects that created the virus in the first place. Dissenting views were quickly censored and silenced everywhere especially in social media. Not only those who promoted a lab origin or genetic engineering origin were silenced but anyone promoting alternative COVID treatment options or dared to question the efficacy and safety of the vaccines. Any views other than that which was promoted by the CDC and the HHS via Fauci were quickly labeled as misinformation. We will focus the "fact-checker" social media campaign censorship further in the next chapter. The aggressive media censorship of a lab origin theory and the silencing of alternative medical treatments for COVID closely resemble the Marxist authoritarian control of public information right out of the Communist Manifesto playbook. Former British Intelligence Richard Dearlove commented on how the propaganda machinery is in line with the CCP: "When you put all of this together, a clear picture emerges: the Chinese Communist Party, assisted by Western scientists with preexisting relationships with China, shaped the global narrative that this was a virus of natural origin from day one."[137]

---

[136] Scott Hounsell, *Wuhan Lab Funder Daszak Emailed Fauci, Thanking Him for Dismissing Lab Leak Theory*. Red State, June 1, 2021. Source accessed January 18, 2022 from https://redstate.com/scotthounsell/2021/06/01/ breaking-wuhan-lab-funder-email-thanks-fauci-for-running-defense-on-lab-leak-theory-n389836.

[137] Markson, *What Really Happened in Wuhan*, 285.

Fauci Faux Pas & Contradictions

Dr. Anthony Fauci established himself through a long career of over fifty years in the public health sector and has held to a significant leadership role in NIAID and NIH. In the eyes of the national public, he has been regarded as "America's Doctor" serving as an advisor to every U.S. president since Ronald Reagan. Fauci came to the forefront of the public spotlight during 2020 as a lead member of the White House Coronavirus Task Force under Trump. The public during a time of fear and uncertainty as they were hunkered down in their homes immediately identified with the doctor in the early outset of the pandemic as being a voice of authority and held onto his every word broadcast on the news networks. Fauci's personal and philosophical worldview is an interesting one. Although Fauci's parents were devout Catholics and he studied in a private Jesuit high school in Manhattan, he eventually distanced himself from religious faith and describes himself as a secular humanist which is a philosophy that believes the greater good for humanity should be accomplished apart from a belief in theism or supernatural belief in religion.[138] In July 2021 Fauci was declared "Humanist of the Year" by the American Humanist Association known for their anti-religious motto "Good Without A God."[139] Jennifer Kalmanson presented the award to Fauci with a glowing tribute: "This is the essence of a scientific mindset and a humanist one...If we are to survive as a species – if we are to overcome the many challenges facing us from this pandemic and the constant threat of new ones on the horizon, to developing a sustainable and just society, to the existential threats of climate change – we must all learn to adapt our thinking and our actions to the best available information." In response to receiving the Humanist of the Year

---

[138] Kennedy, *The Real Anthony Fauci*, 26.

[139] Jennifer Kalmanson, *The Humanist*, October 12, 2021.Source accessed January 19, 2022, from https://thehumanist.com/magazine/fall-2021/features/2021-humanist-of-the-year-dr-anthony-s-fauci

Award, Fauci briefly recounted the story of his education in a Jesuit school but affirmed his departure from faith: My outlook has since evolved to align with the concept of making the world a better place rather than being involved with any organized religion.

The Brooklyn doctor's demeanor exudes with self-confidence, and he is known for his sharp and assertive confrontational manner. This often resulted in tense and awkward moments especially when contradicting President Trump in front of the media. During a March 2020 press conference with Pompeo on Trump's left and Fauci standing slightly behind Trump to his right, a video went viral when Fauci is seen putting his hand over his mouth and snickering at Trump's remarks when he called the State Department the "Deep State Department." The Washington Post's Yasmeen Abutaleb, Health Policy Journalist and Damian Paletta, Economics Editor described Fauci's reaction: "Fauci had been a federal employee for fifty-two years. The doctor's left hand immediately went to his forehead to cover his face. He seemed to be stifling something, a snicker, or a scowl. The whole world saw it. The doctor didn't utter a word, but it was a classic New York 'tell.'... The image ricocheted around the world, appearing on newswires and front pages everywhere."[140] The press conference incident was telling of Fauci's disdain for Trump's conservative leadership style which he considered it a joke. The doctor's cynical attitude would soon speak volumes in the months ahead through the way that would sarcastically "talk down" to those who questioned him.

It also was apparent that while Trump was positive and upbeat about the pandemic and that America was going to come through strong and resilient, and life would return to normal, Fauci on the other hand focused more upon COVID as an existential threat in the worst-case scenario requiring the nation to resort to lockdowns and mandates. In 2021 Fauci was appointed to serve as Biden's chief medical advisor for pandemic response. Later that year conservative

---

[140] Abutalem and Paletta, *Nightmare Scenario*, 154.

Republican senators such as Rand Paul, Tom Cotton, and Ted Cruz have challenged Fauci with the need for greater accountability with not only the way the nation's pandemic response was handled but also for transparency into the GOFR with Wuhan and the NIH. Fauci in an interview with Margaret Brennan on CBS's Face the Nation was asked about the criticism that he had been receiving for his handling of the pandemic. The doctor in a self-assured response resorted to his conventional accusations of anti-science: "Anybody who's looking at this carefully realizes that there's a distinct anti-science flavor to this...They're really criticizing science because I represent science — that's dangerous."[141] While Fauci asserted his authoritarian role as the representative of science, his contradictory statements vacillated considerably in terms of masking, quarantines, and social distancing.

For example, earlier in the outset of the pandemic, Fauci made statements that masks were not necessary. In a February 5, 2020, email he explained to the HHS Secretary Sylvia Burwell the futility of wearing masks: "A mask is more appropriate for someone who is infected and you're trying to prevent them from infecting other people than it is in protecting you against infection. If you look at the masks that you buy in a drug store, the leakage around doesn't really do much to protect you. Now in the United States, there is absolutely no reason whatsoever to wear a mask."[142] This is a reasonable assumption given that ordinary cloth masks are not practical in preventing infection and only those who are sick should wear them in public and not those who are well. The NIH website even has posted information about 52 studies that masks do not reduce viral infection rates. And on February 17, 2020 Fauci told USA Today in an interview, "Now in the United States, there is absolutely

[141] Hannah Grossman, *Ted Cruz Shreds Fauci Delusions Over His I Represent Science Remark*. November 29, 2021. Source accessed January 19, 2022 from https://www.foxnews.com/media / ted-cruz-anthony-fauci-represent-science-remarks-most-dangerous-bureaucrat

[142] Kennedy, *The Real Anthony Fauci*, 52-53.

no reason whatsoever to wear a mask."[143] And to underscore Fauci's statement, the Surgeon General also tweeted: "Seriously people – STOP BUYING MASKS! They are NOT effective in preventing general public from catching #Coronavirus, but if healthcare providers can't get them to care for sick patients, it puts them and our communities at risk."[144] Later in March 2020 Fauci mentioned that the only benefit derived from wearing masks was purely psychological as it had an effect upon "making people feel a little better." If the doctor's statements did not encourage mask wearing in the outset of the pandemic, then why did he later shift to endorsing them? Robert Kennedy, Jr. believes that the shift was politically motivated: "Dr. Fauci's switch to endorsing masks after first recommending against them came at a time of increasing political polarization, and masks quickly became important tribal badges – signals of rectitude for those who embraced Dr. Fauci, and the stigmata of blind obedience to undeserving authority among those who balked."[145] I would also add to Kennedy's statement that mask mandates would be a means to further government control over a free American Republic; there was not any hard and fast scientific evidence available that supported the efficacy of masks. Kennedy further added: "Regional analysis in the United States does not show that [mask] mandates had any effect on case rates, despite 93 percent compliance. Moreover, according to CDC data, 85 percent of people who contracted COVID-19 reported wearing a mask." Also, during seasonal flu season even when there were spikes in influenza cases nationwide, no such mandates for wearing masks were ever implemented. I believe that the mask mandates were implemented entirely for government control. The same thing can be said of social distancing protocols. The former FDA Commissioner Dr. Scott Gotlieb declared that the six-foot distancing rule that Dr. Fauci imposed was "arbitrary," and not supported by scientific evidence.

---

[143] Abutalem and Paletta, *Nightmare Scenario*, 177.

[144] Ibid.

[145] Kennedy, *The Real Anthony Fauci*, 54.

Another inaccurate component was the data modeling that was used by Fauci to estimate the number of COVID-19 deaths. The data was flawed with U.S. death estimates exceeding 525 percent. This huge discrepancy in data is due to the fact that Fauci's model originally predicted 2.2 million deaths. However, only 352,000 deaths were reported in 2020, the difference was 1.848 million deaths, or a 525% overestimation of deaths related to COVID-19 based on models used to project lockdown mandates.[146] According to Kennedy Neal Ferguson from the Imperial College of London worked with $148.8 million in funding from Bill and Melinda Gates Foundation to develop this so-called pandemic data projection analysis system. Fauci who is in lockstep with the Gates Foundation utilized this system to justify lockdowns in the U.S. More inaccuracy also resulted in the way that death certificates were recorded to reflect a higher death rate due to COVID. Fauci used the death rate data to inflate the number of deaths while later the CDC admitted that only 6 percent of total COVID deaths occurred in healthy individuals. The reporting lacked objective comorbidity data. Yet, the CDC decided to skip autopsies from deaths attributed to adverse effects from the vaccine. These inaccuracies were further exacerbated through the flawed HHS VAERS surveillance system for vaccine in not reporting of adverse reactions by as much as 99 percent. All the flawed data and contradictions that Fauci made during the pandemic were nothing more than a premeditated means for mandating control over the American people. Kennedy states: "All of Dr. Fauci's intrusive mandates and his deceptive use of data tended to stoke fear and amplify desperation for the anticipated arrival of vaccines that would transfer billions of dollars from taxpayers to pharmaceutical executives and shareholders."[147] The contradictions and the bureaucratic mandates that Fauci issued were troubling enough but

---

[146] Kennedy, *The Real Anthony Fauci*, 54.

[147] Ibid, 60.

the web of entanglement with Bioweapons would prove to be even more alarming.

The Murky Relationship Between
HHS, NIH, & CDC with Bioweapons Technology

The United States began its military research and development of offensive bioweapons during World War II under the Roosevelt Administration in 1943. The U.S. Army Biological Warfare Laboratories (USBWL) at Fort Detrick ran top secret programs partnering with phar-maceutical industry giant Merck. The USBWL eventually shifted its research to "medical" GOFR projects and became USAMRIID (U.S. Army Medical Research Institute of Infectious Diseases) under the command of David Franz who would provide leadership for the next twenty-three years. Franz's role would be significant in the GOFR projects for Fauci and the Pentagon with the study of Coronaviruses. There was limited support for this scope of research until after the 2001 anthrax attacks then under George Bush there was a renewed focus upon a modern "Biosecurity Program." It is then with the issue of Homeland Security Presidential Directive 21 (HSPD-21) that HHS,

NIH, and the CDC would develop programs for bioterrorism preparedness.[148] This directive is what initiated funding for my previous career
as a bioterrorism emergency preparedness planner. In August of 2017
retired U.S. Airforce bioweapons expert Col. Robert P. Kadlec came to
serve as The Assistant Secretary of Health and Human Services (HHS)
for the Preparedness and Response Division until January 2021. Kadlec
aggressively promoted planning for emerging biological threats with
infectious diseases and the need for a militarized response for national
security and preparedness. Recall in Chapter Four our discussion of
the HHS proposal set forth during the pause on GOFR projects titled
*Framework for Guiding Funding Decisions About Proposed Research
Involving Enhanced Potential Pandemic Pathogens.* This important
document focused on "potential pandemic pathogens" referred to
as "PPP's" and made the case for resuming GOFR funding. Kadlec
worked closely with Fauci on the committees for this guidance with
the intent of resuming the NIH research on Coronaviruses.[149] When the
GOFR projects resumed after the temporary pause in funding, Kadlec
and Fauci worked through the NIAID, the NIH and the Biomedical
Advanced Research Development Authority (BARDA). BARDA under
the HHS Preparedness and Response Program describes its mission
for Medical Countermeasures as to "provide an integrated, systematic
approach to the development of necessary vaccines, drugs, therapies
for pandemics and emerging infectious diseases."[150] Millions of dollars
of funding were being distributed for GOFR projects to include Wuhan
along with the NIH. Kadlec created strategy planning for the Pentagon
for the development and use of pandemic pathogens as a stealth bioweapon capable of leaving no trace and stated: "Biological weapons

---

[148] George W. Bush, *Homeland Security Presidential Directive 21; Public Health &
Medical Preparedness.* Source accessed January 20, 2022, from https://irp.fas.
org/offdocs/nspd/hspd-21.htm.

[149] Kennedy, *The Real Anthony Fauci,* 793.

[150] Biomedical Advanced Research Development Authority website: https://www.
medicalcountermeasures.gov/BARDA.

under the cover of an endemic or natural disease occurrence pro-vides an attacker the potential for plausible denial. Biological war-fare's potential to create significant economic losses and consequent political instability, coupled with plausible deniability, exceeds the possibilities of any other human weapon."[151] Kadlec gives a powerful description of the devastating power of a bioweapon: "significant eco-nomic losses and political instability." The COVID pandemic's impact matches Kadlec's description regarding the effects of a bioweapon.

Between 2001 and 2014 the U.S. spent approximately $80 billion on biodefense. Because of restrictions under the Biological Weapons Convention, research had to reflect more of a medical perspective rather than an offensive weapons program. Therefore, such changes as the name "Biological Warfare Lab" to "Medical Research Institute of Infectious Diseases" sounded less hostile and tended toward a more humanitarian purpose. The same strategy to call for resuming GOFR project funding was used by Fauci and Collins before the May 17, 2017 House Appropriations Committee to put their research in a more pos-itive light to benefit humanitarian research. To further sustain biode-fense research in this context a more congenial directive under Vice President Cheney was to transfer the research programs from the Department of Defense to the NIH and to the National Institute of Allergy and Infectious Diseases (NIAID). When this transfer was com-pleted in 2004, Fauci became extensively aligned with the bioweapons research program. Under Fauci, NIAID received $1.7 billion in funding. Kennedy adds: "the NIAID Strategic Plan for Biodefense Research and the NIAID Biodefense Research Agenda for CDC Category A agents, which were those microorganisms designated by CDC to be poten-tial pandemic pathogens – these were used to brand contagions as pressing terror threats, drum up pandemic panic, and lobby for gov-ernment support for NIAID's new battery of biodefense vaccinations."[152]

---

[151] Kennedy, *The Real Anthony Fauci*, 794.

[152] Ibid, 818.

Another military research agency that had ties with NIH and EcoHealth was the Defense Advanced Research Project Agency (DARPA). DARPA has funded military defense technology projects since the time of the Sputnik satellite in the 1950's, and they implemented the very first internet system along with stealth bombers and pilotless drones. The agency also is credited with creating data mining systems in phone communication surveillance for the NSA but when this was abandoned due to public scrutiny the technology later helped to launch Facebook. This connection with social media platforms came about when DARPA's former director Dr. Regina Dugan moved to Google as an executive but later transferred to work on projects for Facebook. But even more significant is DARPA's role in the COVID pandemic. Their website details their projects with the Department of Defense and multiple government agencies and academic institutions regarding the COVID-19 pandemic.[153] DARPA references their work with Detect It With Gene Editing Technologies (DIGET) which are a primary component of GOFR. The agency also provides a brief description of their "manufacture of medical countermeasures to combat COVID-19" by explaining: "DARPA technology contributes to preventing future COVID-19 infections through novel vaccine technology." DARPA mentions that this technology was developed using "influenza, Zika, and MERS as test cases." According to Kennedy in addition to funding GOFR projects at Fort Detrick and financing key technologies for the Moderna vaccine, DARPA has also channeled $6.5 million through Daszak's EcoHealth Alliance for experimental research at the Wuhan Lab.[154] All of this tangled web between the military, the HHS, NIH, EcoHealth, and Wuhan with bioweapons technology leads up to an even bigger picture in creating a crisis – the COVID-19 pandemic for a "global reset."

---

[153] Defense Advanced Research Projects Agency (DARPA); COVID, March 19, 2021. Website: https://www.darpa. mil/work-with-us/covid-19.

[154] Kennedy, *The Real Anthony Fauci*, 847.

CHAPTER 6

A CONVENIENT CRISIS
FOR THE GLOBAL RESET

Governments do like epidemics, just the same way as they like war, really. It's a chance to impose their will on us and get us all scared so that we huddle together and do what we're told. – Dr. Damien Downing, President, British Society of Ecological Medicine

Nothing Spreads Like Fear

The movie *Contagion* released in 2011 is a medical thriller about a global pandemic that originates in Hong Kong through a deadly novel respiratory virus resulting from Avian (bird) flu crossover to humans through the local meat markets. In my former line of work just prior to the release of the movie, I met one of the technical consultants for the film in a conference meeting who was working as a quarantine officer with the CDC. The producers were inspired by the 2002 SARS outbreak and consulted with medical experts from WHO and CDC to develop a realistic narrative. At the time I was a senior emergency preparedness planner in local government and our team was in the process of reviewing various national pandemic response plans. My team was curious to see how realistic the movie scenario was, so we went to see the film. Several of us had epidemiological and medical backgrounds in our profession and thought it would be an interesting

117

opportunity to see how Hollywood portrayed a pandemic. One of the central characters of the film was "Dr. Ellis Cheever" a chief epidemiologist with the CDC played by Laurence Fishburne. When Dr. Cheever was asked if he thought that the virus was weaponized as a terrorist bioweapon, he replied that "Someone doesn't have to weaponize it, the birds are doing that" which is eerily reminiscent the zoonotic origins theory espoused by Dr. Fauci and the WHO for COVID. As the movie narrative plays out the deadly pathogen spreads out of control. Soon chaos and civil disorder ensue as National Guard are deployed to lock down entire states in mass quarantine as the U.S. president and vice president goes to underground bunkers. Along with grim scenes of mass burial graves we also see closed businesses and airports, empty store shelves, rioting and looting as fear and mayhem are rampant everywhere. The hero of the movie Dr. Cheever and the CDC "save the world" with the introduction of a newly developed vaccine. Once the vaccine is developed, the government closely controls the distribution of the vaccine. While the film was not a big blockbuster (it made $136.5 million), it had an incredible resurgence in 2020 and was watched by millions who were hunkered down in their homes during COVID. A movie poster which advertised *Contagion* in big bold letters read, *Nothing Spreads Like Fear."* Strangely enough the fictional Hollywood narrative that was produced a mere nine years prior to the COVID pandemic had some striking similarities to what we have witnessed, especially fear. When individuals succumb to fear, they easily give up their cherished liberties, personal rights, and individual freedoms. Like the scenes that play right out of the movie *Contagion,* businesses, schools, and churches close as we become fearful of a dreaded plague, and we become compliant with government mandates as the media and major news networks become harbingers of dread. What is amazing about the screen plot's work of fiction, is that a similar narrative has served as the basis for government exercises, drills, and trainings in our National Response Plan (NRP) for many years even before the film debuted in theaters!

Pandemic Exercise & Response Planning Scenarios

Government planning utilizes HSEEP (Homeland Security Exercise Evaluation Protocols) for developing emergency response plans for every possible scenario from natural disasters to pandemics. This is also part of what is referred to as the National Response Framework (NRF) that establishes the procedures for Incident Management and dictate Incident Command Systems (ICS) for first responders in military, fire, law enforcement, health and medical. Federal response planning rolls out fifteen distinct categories that are specific for every emergency scenario. These are called Emergency Service

Functions (ESF's). ESF-8 is the planning category for health and medical emergency response. It is ESF-8 that covers everything from mass fatalities to pandemics. As a senior emergency preparedness planner in local government over the course of twenty years in my previous career I wrote dozens of planning annexes and standard operating procedures also within health and medical as my specialized areas were in public health epidemiology and bioterrorism. For every emergency response plan that I wrote, it did not merely go on the shelf to collect dust. Rather we were required by HSEEP standards to "test" the plans through drills and exercises with government officials and stakeholders. Either fictional scenarios or incidents based on real-life occurrences would provide the basis for a training simulation.

The exercises were coordinated as a "table-top" where the participants were gathered in a conference room setting for discussion or as
an actual training exercise practiced by "event actors." The scenario
that played out in *Contagion* included every conceivable scenario that
is included in government plans for pandemic response and exercises:
deadly outbreaks, deaths, mass hysteria, civil chaos, supply shortages,
media and social media information campaigns, isolation and quarantine, vaccine deployment and government mandates. The Federal
Emergency Management Agency (FEMA) has exercise and planning
templates for pandemics that can be downloaded online. These templates were made available for government Continuity Operations
Planning (COOP) Units through the Department of Homeland Security
(DHS). FEMA pandemic response planning guidance listed a "Summary
of Federal Government Planning Assumptions" which included specific areas such as "absenteeism will fluctuate between 30-40%
during peaks of the pandemic waves and the factor of "asymptomatic infected persons who can transmit infection and develop immunity to subsequent infection."[155] I personally was involved in dozens of
these government exercises. Sometimes for the large regional exercises that incorporated multiple federal and state agencies we would
hire professional consultants to assist with the planning and the mod-
eration of the exercise. For one such pandemic exercise we hired an
individual who later became one of the earlier FEMA directors in the
Trump Administration. I also coordinated an exercise that focused on
the containment of a high consequence disease pathogens (HCID's),
at the DFW International Airport which utilized various law enforcement agencies to "lock down" and quarantine an entire jet plane with
passengers and crew. For every exercise that was conducted a "situation manual" also known as a SITMAN was utilized as the fictional
scenario that drove the planned components of the "exercise script."
After each exercise we would conduct a thorough "After-Action"

---

[155] Federal Emergency Management Agency (FEMA), *Exercise Determined Accord:
Influenza Pandemic TTX for Continuity Managers*, 2007.

report and develop a specific "incident-action plan" (IAP) objectives to improve agency response capabilities in accordance with DHS and FEMA standards. The public has very little awareness of these pandemic exercises conducted in military, federal, and local government agencies. And just prior to the COVID pandemic many of these exercises were conducted with incredible detail as if it were one big "dress rehearsal" for 2020.

"Plandemic" Exercises with Powerful Global Elites

Powerful nonprofit organizations and foundations have funneled billions of dollars into the forefront of not only pandemic exercises and response planning, but also the development of vaccines through relationships with big corporate pharmaceutical giants. The Bill and Melinda Gates Foundation (BMGF) has played a significant role before and after the COVID pandemic. Their website reflects their globalist aspirations regarding the pandemic: "There is no such thing as a national solution to a global crisis...A global response must also aim to build more reliant health systems that can quickly identify emerging outbreaks and help protect the world's most vulnerable people."[156] The Foundation sets forth very humanitarian statements describing its work as a concern for the public health of the global community during COVID as it mentions that it has given more than "$2 billion in contributions since the pandemic began, we are working on strategic long-term initiatives, including efforts to address barriers to gender equality and ensure an inclusive and equitable economic recovery." A significant Gates partner has been John Hopkins University which has been in the forefront of pandemic exercise preparedness. Starting with over $20 million in funding for the Institute for the Johns Hopkins Population and Reproductive Health in 1999 which advocates global population control, Gates has since contributed vast streams of funding to the institution for a series

---

[156] Bill & Melinda Gates Foundation website: https://www.gatesfoundation.

of pandemic exercise simulations.[157] In the last chapter we mentioned Col. Kadlec who worked with the DOD, NIH, and CDC along with Fauci to develop biological weapons strategic planning. Gates also partnered with Kadlec for pandemic exercise simulations and other deals emerged from NIH and NIAID to fund Hopkins with over $13 billion since 2001. The simulations that Gates had developed through John Hopkins along with NIH focused on the use of police powers to detain and quarantine citizens, the imposition of martial law, control of media, censorship, mask mandates, lockdowns, vaccination deployment, and contact trace surveillance for pandemics. Kennedy mentions that biological weapons expert Tara O'Toole is the co-founder of the John Hopkins Center for Civilian Biodefense Studies as well as the vice president of a bio-technology corporation that works closely with funding projects for the CIA known as "In-Q-Tel."[158] Their web site describes their work which is a "convergence of the digital world with biology."[159] In-Q-Tel has close allies among the corporate giants of "Silicon Valley": Microsoft, Facebook, Google and PayPal. Gates has utilized his connections in each of these corporations to leverage pandemic response planning along with long term investment strategies.

Gates along with partners through John Hopkins conducted pandemic simulation exercises before COVID which included the advent of a dystopian age where societies live under the grim reality of continuous viral pathogen variants which they term as the "New Normal." Many of these exercises included components for "militarizing medicine and introducing centralized autocratic governance."[160] They featured training scenarios for what was called "mass prophylaxis" which was a term for distributing vaccines and viral antidotes at large distribution sites called "Point of Dispensing Sites" (PODS). Many of

---

[157] Kennedy, *The Real Anthony Fauci*, 796.

[158] Ibid, 802.

[159] In-Q-Tel: *COVID-19 Efforts in B.Next*. Site: https://www. bnext.org

[160] Kennedy, *The Real Anthony Fauci*, 838 & 845.

these exercise scenarios were also rolled out through public health emergency preparedness programs (PHEP) which received millions of dollars of funding from the CDC for local county, city, and state health departments. In 2010 when the WHO implemented biosecurity planning for the management of global risks, Gates also delivered a speech titled "Decade of Vaccines" to the U.N. on biosecurity. At the same time another leader among the global elites, Peter Schwartz who is described as a "think-tank futurist" has also come to the forefront in pandemic response planning exercises. Schwartz is a global socialist who as a university student was a member of the "Students for a Democratic Society" a left-leaning activist organization. His background includes the utilization of scenario planning based upon strategic military research and development models conducted by RAND. His background proved to be a complimentary component for exercise and simulation development. Schwartz also ran the Stanford Research Institute's Strategic Environment Center which was known to host the CIA's psychological warfare program research known as "MKUltra" that included the strategic use of propaganda, torture, and psychiatric chemicals to control societies. Schwartz created the "Global Business Network" in 1987 in Berkeley which includes subject matter experts from various fields such as media, global economy, and biotechnology.

Schwartz was funded by the Rockefeller Foundation for a scenario report he created in 2010 also in partnership with his Global Business Network (GBN) called "Scenarios for the Future of Technology and International Development." The Rockefeller Foundation is another elite organization that invests billions of dollars into socialist global strategies such as the "Pandemic Prevention Institute" which aims to "strengthen global surveillance capability."[161] In Schwartz's report that he authored for the Rockefeller Foundation he addresses a pandemic scenario under a section called *Lock Step* in which he advocates the following principle for pandemic resilience: "A world of tighter top-down government control and more authoritarian leadership, with limited innovation and growing citizen pushback."[162] The specific scenario that is used in the report regards a "new influenza strain (*from zoonotic origins*) that was extremely virulent and deadly." Schwartz' pandemic scenario plays out with an infection rate of twenty percent and a death rate of eight million of the world's population impacting economies and supply chains. Most interesting is that the scenario highlights that China did better than most free world nations and the U.S. in surviving the pandemic because "The Chinese government's quick imposition and enforcement of mandatory quarantine for all citizens, as well as its instant and near-hermetic sealing off of all borders, saved millions of lives, stopping the spread of the virus far earlier than in other countries and enabling a swifter post-pandemic recovery." In his scenario, Schwartz praises the Communist Chinese government and other authoritarian nations for their implementation of rigid authoritarian control in defeating the virus and their citizen's willingness to submit to these controls: "Citizens were more tolerant, and even eager, for top-down direction and oversight, and national leaders had more

---

[161] Rockefeller Foundation Web Site – *Preventing Future Pandemics*: https://www.rockefellerfoundation.org

[162] Peter Schwartz, *Scenarios for the Future of Technology and International Development*, May 2010. Produced by the Rockefeller Foundation & Global Business Network, 18.

latitude to impose order in the ways they saw fit. In developed countries, this heightened oversight took many forms: biometric IDs for all citizens...In many developed countries, enforced cooperation with a suite of new regulations and agreements slowly but steadily restored both order and, importantly, economic growth." What Schwartz is presenting in his pandemic scenario is that greater government control will be needed to include "biometric ID's" for every citizen and "new regulations to restore order." For Schwartz, government control and more of it will be needed for pandemic recovery and he also asserts that the "citizens will be more tolerant and more eager for this top-down" government oversight. He also criticized those nations that were inclined to a greater degree of national sovereignty: "virulent nationalism created new hazards...The U.S. and EU struck back with retaliatory national standards, throwing a wrench in the development and diffusion of technology globally." Schwartz's pandemic scenario principles have remarkable similarities to the actual practices of government overreach and control that we witnessed during the 2020-2022 COVID pandemic through mask and vaccine mandates and closures. However, Schwartz is known for his uncanny ability to create these fictional scenarios and then have them to later play out in real world events. In 2000 he submitted a study for a Senate commission where he "predicted the horrifying possibility of terrorists flying planes into the World Trade Center."[163] In 2004 his GBN was testing strategies for major airlines to survive a Coronavirus pandemic. Schwartz's fictional scenarios becoming real world incidents are either an incredible coincidence or there is something sinister behind these scenarios that predict the future. More scenarios at a global scale unfolded in the following years that had amazing similarities to the actual COVID pandemic.

---

[163] Kennedy, *The Real Anthony Fauci*, 851.

Global Exercises or Dress Rehearsals?

After 2010 Fauci and Gates led the globalist biosecurity agenda through partnerships with military and intelligence for the development of successive follow up pandemic simulations especially in the U.S. Later in 2017 Gates worked with the health ministries of the world's wealthiest G20 nations to conduct in a joint exercise scenario that included China as the center of a deadly outbreak with the fictitious name "Mountain Associated Respiratory Virus" or its acronym "MARS" which is also known as the Roman god of war.[164] The global exercise included the Gates Foundation and other elite institutions such as the Rockefeller Foundation, the World Bank and the WHO. Interestingly enough, the French company BioMerieux that built the Wuhan lab, along with representatives from China participated in the simulation. One of the moderators of the exercise who worked closely with the Gates Foundation was David Heymann who is also CEO of Moderna that later developed the COVID vaccines. The second moderator was Professor Ilona Kickbusch a member of Gate's Global Preparedness Monitoring Board for pandemics. The exercise scenario played out with amazing similarities to Schwartz's Lockstep scenario with tight government-controlled lockdowns and concluded with the WHO coordinating an orchestrated global response which brought the fictional MARS pandemic to an end.

A few months later in October of 2017 a tabletop exercise was developed by Gates and conducted at the Johns Hopkins Center for Health Security which is their global biosecurity command center. The NIH and NIAID along with the Gates Foundation were the primary funders of the exercise. The scenario titled "SPARS 2017" featured a fictional coronavirus pandemic that ran its course for three years. This scenario that unfolded regarded the origin of the coronavirus as being from a bioterrorist attack rather than a zoonotic

---

[164] Kennedy, *The Real Anthony Fauci*, 853.

origin. The exercise included scenario injects where mass vaccina-
tion operations were planned like a "wargame." SPARS exercise participants role-played authoritarian governmental control to mitigate
the pandemic to include media, surveillance, censorship, and political control. The eighty-nine-page exercise situation manual rolled out
a month by month play of pandemic events that bear striking similarity to the COVID pandemic. It is an interesting coincidence that
three years after the exercise the Senior Analyst at Johns Hopkins
Center for Health Security where the exercise was hosted would be
the one who would discover the first U.S. case of COVID. It was not too
long afterwards when Gates was celebrating the success of the SPARS
simulated exercise, he delivered a speech at the Malaria Summit in
London on April 18, 2018. At the summit Gates warned nineteen
British Commonwealth countries "that a deadly new disease could
arise within a decade, taking the world by surprise, spreading globally
and killing tens of millions."[165] Using the same "wargame" approach
from the SPARS exercise in 2017 he exhorted the audience in London:
"The world needs to prepare for pandemics in the same serious way
that it prepares for war."

---

[165] Ibid, 861.

On May 15, 2018, the Johns Hopkins Center for Health Security conducted in Washington, D.C. a pandemic/biowarfare preparedness exercise titled "Clade X."[166] This exercise included a fictional bioengineered pathogen that produces a novel virus for which there is no human immunity. The Clade X scenario plays out with over 100 million deaths globally along with a U.S. Stock Market crash. The National Security Council played a prominent role in the exercise which emphasized the need for a militarized pandemic response as well as strategies for media and social media control. Clade X also featured school and business closures as hospitals were overwhelmed as they exceeded surge capacity and the need for the rapid deployment of vaccines. The event livestreamed on Facebook to guests by closed invitation only. Amazon CEO Jeff Bezos shortly after buying the Washington Post on September 19, 2018 for $250 million gave a reporter a foreboding remark of the Clade X exercise: "This mock pandemic killed 150 million people. Next time it might not be a drill." The well-orchestrated pandemic scenarios that Gates had been rolling out utilized sophisticated data modeling programs that his foundation developed through the "Institute for Disease Modeling" (IDM). The IDM website states its purpose: "To support global efforts to eradicate infectious diseases and achieve permanent improvements in health by developing, using, and sharing computational modeling tools and promoting quantitative decision-making…Disease modeling benefits the entire global health community by providing new insight into old problems, testing novel combinations of strategies, and enabling the collection of more valuable data in the field."[167] According to Kennedy the IDM data which provided exaggerated estimates that 22 million people could die of COVID within the first 12 months, would be used by Fauci to push the

---

[166] Ibid, 864-867.

[167] Institute for Disease Modeling, Bill & Melinda Gates Foundation. https://www.gatesfoundation.org/our-work/programs/global-health/ Institute-for-Disease-Modeling

need for lockdowns and mandates.[168] The pandemic modeling scenarios developed prior to the COVID pandemic reinforced Gate's message that such a global pandemic was inevitable and that mandatory vaccines would be needed to mitigate the outbreak.

Another global organization that was created in May 2018 by the World Bank and the WHO that has further utilized the after-action review process of these pandemic exercise scenarios is the Global Preparedness Monitoring Board (GPMB). The GPMB web site proclaims that it is "comprised of political leaders, agency principals and world-class experts" for the purpose of "accelerating research and development to enhance global and regional coordination capabilities."[169] Their site adds a press release from WHO titled: "WHO and World Bank Group join forces to strengthen global health security." The article speaks of Dr. Jim Yong Kim the president of World Bank and the partnership with WHO to "strengthen global health security through stringent independent monitoring and regular preparedness to tackle outbreaks, pandemics and other emergencies with health consequences." Dr. Kim an American Democratic Party loyalist who is listed in Forbes Magazine as "One of the World's Most Powerful People" was nominated for the World Bank Presidency by Barack Obama in 2012. The GPMB includes some of the most influential leaders in the global public health community that create international health policies. Among this elite group within the GPMB is Fauci and China's CDC Director George Gao. In less than twenty weeks before the public declaration of the COVID pandemic the GPMB released a report warning that "we are entering a new phase of high impact epidemics that would constitute the new normal where governments worldwide would strengthen control and restrict the mobility of citizens."[170]

---

[168] Kennedy, *The Real Anthony Fauci*, 867-868

[169] Global Preparedness Monitoring Board, *About Us*. https://www.gpmb.org/about-us

[170] Kennedy, *The Real Anthony Fauci*, 871.

Within the same period that the GPMB was releasing their reports on the inevitability of a global viral plague, two more realistic COVID-like pandemic simulations are launched just months prior to the COVID pandemic. In August of 2019 a secretive war game code named "Crimson Contagion" was led by Kadlec Director of Biodefense, along with Fauci representing the NIH, Robert Redfield, CDC Director, and HHS Secretary Alex Azar.[171] The exercise focused on simulation drills for engagement of multi-level federal and state public health agencies along with law enforcement agencies. The simulation involved a novel influenza virus called H7N9 that originated from China. In the scenario just like what had happened in the actual COVID pandemic, the HHS secretary declares the outbreak as a pandemic while the WHO delays the declaration. There were drills associated with the exercise that included social distancing and deployment of vaccine as a medical countermeasure. The after-action-report emphasized the need for an aggressive implementation of social distancing and strictly enforced closures as a means of mitigating the pandemic. Just a mere three months after Crimson Contagion was conducted, Gates directed a global exercise called "Event 201" in October 2019. This exercise comes right on the heels of China's Coronavirus pandemic exercise at the Wuhan Airport in September 2019 and occurs during the World Military Games in Wuhan in October 2019 as well. Event 201 included four tabletop exercises of a global Coronavirus pandemic. Participants from the World Bank, the World Economic Forum (which we shall talk more later about Klaus Schwab), Bloomberg, Forbes, Johns Hopkins, the CDC, the People's Republic of China, CIA, NSA, and pharmaceutical giant Johnson & Johnson that later developed COVID vaccines. Were all these powerful global elites aware of the GOFR experiments going on in the Wuhan Lab with the deliberate engineering of SARS-CoV-2? The timing of the Event 201 tabletop simulations was incredibly close to the time that we believe the actual events were transpiring in

---

[171] Ibid, 871-874.

Wuhan. The tabletop scenarios included role playing of a "Pandemic Control Council" which sought to control media narratives, issue mask mandates, and promote mass vaccinations. All the exercise simulations over a course of several years prior to the COVID pandemic have amazing similarities to the actual pandemic in the way that events played out in 2020. If there ever was a case for the conspiracy accusations of a so-called *Plandemic* the pre-COVID exercise simulations would be incredibly convincing. However, the most compelling character of all time who is not merely the imagination of a conspiracy scheme, has been quite forthcoming in their admissions for the grand opportunity behind the COVID pandemic – Klaus Schwab who wrote about it in his book.

The Great Reset

Klaus Schwab is the founder and executive chairman of the World Economic Forum (WEF) that is headquartered in Geneva, Switzerland and has offices in San Francisco and New York. The purpose of the WEF is stated on their website: "The World Economic Forum LLC is committed to improving the state of the world by engaging industry, government and civil society leaders in partnerships to shape global, regional and industry agendas."[172] Schwab is a global economist who advocates what is known as "Stakeholder Capitalism" which is a socialist model for economic development that centers upon the planet (eco-conservatism) and its people: "The planet is thus the center of the global economic system, and its health should be optimized in the decisions made by all other stakeholders."[173] This concept is contrasted with "shareholder capitalism" which Schwab says

[172] World Economic Forum LLC, *About*. https://www.weforum.org/ /about/ world-economic-forum-llc

[173] "What is Stakeholder Capitalism? *Global Agenda – Klaus Schwab*. https://www.weforum.org/agenda/2021/01/klaus-schwab -on-what-is-stakeholder-capitalism-history-relevance/

is the norm for Western capitalism in markets by maximizing short-term profits in competitive market free economy. It becomes apparent that the only thing that even remotely resembles capitalism is the term itself used in "shareholder capitalism" by Schwab. The scope of his socialist economic principles comes to light through his works on *The Fourth Industrial Revolution* which is characterized by the convergence of nanotechnology and biotechnology platforms. This economic theory resembles the Soviet "Industrial Revolution that was a Marxist-Leninist axiom that a socialist society must rest on an industrial base."[174] Schwab's premise that "Innovations in the biological ream – genetics in particular...As research into genetic engineering progresses (for example, the development of the Clustered Regularly Interspaced Short Palindromic Repeats (CRISPR/Cas9) method in gene editing are the backdrop for this "Fourth Industrial Revolution."[175] CRISPR technology edits genes by precisely cutting DNA and letting it interact with natural DNA sequences. While there is potential for this technology to be applied to fight diseases like cancer, there is another application where it can also be used in engineering deadly pathogens. It is an interesting coincidence that one of the very tenets of GOFR research which led to the creation of the SARS-CoV-2 virus – genetic engineering is espoused by Schwab. He maintains that industrial revolution brings about radical change and is a major departure from conventional economic models by utilization of new technologies on a global scale for the good of humanity and the planet.

Schwab likens COVID-19 to the Great plague in Europe in the Middle Ages in its power to shape and to change societies: "If such profound social, political and economic changes could be provoked by the plague in the medieval world, could the COVID-19 pandemic mark the onset of a similar turning point with long-lasting and dramatic

---

[174] Pipes, *Communism; A History*, 58.

[175] Klaus Schwab, *The Forth Industrial Revolution*. https://www.academia.edu/35846430/ The_Fourth_Industrial_Revolution_Klaus_Schwab.

consequences for our world today?"[176] The "turning point" that Schwab is contemplating will "accelerate systemic change" in sovereign nationalism to globalism. Here he wholeheartedly endorses the pandemic as the means to achieve this globalist utopia: "we should take advantage of this unprecedented opportunity to reimagine our world, in a bid to make it a better and a more resilient one as it emerges from the other side of the crisis." It is of little surprise that Schwab who participated in Gates global Event 201 exercise speaks highly of the global agenda for pandemic preparedness: "For years, international organizations like the World Health Organization (WHO), institutions like the World Economic Forum and the Coalition for Epidemic Preparedness Innovations (CEPI – launched at the Annual Meeting 2017 in Davos), and individuals like Bill Gates have been warning us about the next pandemic." The global organization CEPI mentioned by Schwab was founded by the Gates Foundation and the British pharmaceutical investor Welcome Trust through a grant of $460 million and launched at the World Economic Forum meeting in Davos, Switzerland. Its goal is to finance research projects for vaccines with its focus upon MERS-CoV and Nipah viral pathogens. Such enterprises as CEPI have been part the World Economic Forum's strategic plan because of the forum's underlying stated assumption: "History shows that epidemics have been the great resitter of countries' economy and social fabric. Why should it be different with COVID-19?"

One of the great changes that Schwab mentions that the pandemic will help usher in will be in the creation of a global currency. He begins by mentioning the "exorbitant privilege" that the U.S. has enjoyed with retaining its currency reserve that will deteriorate due to inflation and federal debt which makes international investors willing to fund it. He criticizes the U.S. for "weaponizing the U.S. dollar for geopolitical purposes by punishing companies that do business with Iran or North Korea." The alternative to a national currency such as the U.S.

---

[176] Schwab & Malleret, *The Great Reset*, 15.

dollar that Schwab proposes is a digital currency that he praises China for testing it in their larger cities. He believes that a digital currency with electronic payment platforms will be the new economic methodology of the future and the pandemic will help to accelerate the world to this end. Schwab further criticizes the U.S. for its "shocking social disparities" which have been magnified in the pandemic especially with low-income populations such as African Americans: "In America as in many other countries, African Americans are poorer, more likely to be unemployed or underemployed and victims of substandard housing and living conditions."[177] He also adds that the "civil unrest" that resulted in the death of George Floyd during the COVID pandemic further exacerbated America's divide between African Americans and white Americans. All of America's racial and social ills are what Schwab describes as being a result of its strong individualistic nationalism: "For this reason, strongly individualistic societies like the U.S. could be more at risk than European or Asian countries that either have a greater sense of solidarity (like in Southern Europe) or a better social system for assisting the underprivileged (like in northern Europe)." What is Schwab's alternative to America's self-centered individualistic nationalism? It is clearly expressed in his section titled *The Return of Big Government*: "In the words of John Micklethwait and Adrian Wooldridge: The COVID-19 pandemic has made government important again...One of the great lessons of the past five centuries in Europe and America is this: acute crisis contribute to boosting the power of the state. It's always been the case and there is no reason why it should be different with the COVID-19 pandemic." One of the problems of the Western world for nations like the U.S. according to Schwab is that "the role of the state has shrunk considerably. This is a situation that is set to change because it is hard to imagine how an exogenous shock of such magnitude as the one inflicted by COVID-19 could be addressed with purely market-based solutions." What Schwab

---

[177] Schwab & Malleret, *The Great Reset*, 73-81.

is saying that American free market capitalism ("market-based solutions) is to blame for its individualistic nationalism and the shrinking role of the state having more power over its citizens.

Schwab believes that the COVID pandemic will be the catalyst for this social-economic revolution that he says is moving further to the left and will be accomplished through big globalist government: "Everything that comes in the post-pandemic era will lead us to rethink government's role...How will this expanded role of governments manifest itself? A significant element of new 'bigger' government is already in place with the vastly increased and quasi-immediate government control of the economy."[178] Schwab firmly believes that the COVID pandemic will be a global game changer and will require that big government will need to rewrite the rules: "Looking to the future, governments will most likely, but with different degrees of intensity, decide that it's in the best interest of society to rewrite some of the rules of the game and permanently increase their role." With a globalist agenda advanced through the pandemic he proposes the redistribution of wealth, higher taxes on the wealthy and the radical implementation of policies such as anti-climate change environmentalism:

---

[178] Schwab & Malleret, *The Great Reset*, 92, 102-103.

"Research and development for global public goods such as health and climate change solutions will be actively pursued. Taxation will increase particularly for the most privileged, because governments will need to strengthen their resilience capabilities and with to invest more heavily in them." Another revolution that will come because of the pandemic will be implemented through social media for the expression of issues represented by climate change, gender equality, and LGBTQ rights – these according to Schwab will be "the catalyst for change and a source of critical momentum for the Great Reset." In the equation of the Great Reset the last enemy to be defeated will be nationalism that will be brought down by anarchy giving way to a new global order. Schwab quotes the late economist Jean-Pierre Lehmann who was an advocate for global governance and a guest lecturer at Johns Hopkins (the university at the forefront of pandemic exercises): "There is no new global order, just a chaotic transition to uncertainty."[179] The chaotic impact of the pandemic has brought uncertainty in the U.S. local and national economies by "adding gasoline to the fire" from a socialist democratic administration through runaway inflation, excessive stock market volatility, and supply chain shortages. The pandemic and a leftist leaning government pushed the nation from a once prosperous economy to what resembles an economically bankrupt socialist state under the draconian mandates for masks and vaccines. American citizens were being terminated by their employers and military personnel were being discharged from active duty for refusing to get COVID vaccines. Big government is using the COVID pandemic for orchestrating a coup d'etat of our constitutional republic. One of the tools of big government for achieving this transition into a socialist society is media censorship and control. Just like in a Communist state, it takes a propaganda of fear to enforce control over its citizens. The globalist reset agenda will be carried out through

---

[179] Schwab, *The Great Reset*, 103-104.

a state-controlled media that will seek to influence the thoughts and opinions of the people.

The Propaganda Tool of the State – the Media

I did not realize how powerful state-controlled media sources were until I worked with local and state governments. At the government level are public information plans known as CERC Plans (Crisis Emergency Risk Communications) also known as "risk communications." In an emergency or a disaster, the CERC plans provide templates for press releases and specific protocols for working with news media and even provide specific guidance on the utilization of social media. The lead individual in both governments and large corporations is know as the "public information officer" or PIO. These persons ensure that the "narrative" is driven in the best interests of the agency. The same protocols are used for the COVID pandemic. Everything from pandemic related business and school closures and mandates to vaccine and testing operations are crafted through the public information office to make certain that it does not deviate from the mainstream media narrative. On COVID matters the PIO will "fact-check" their media content through the sounding board of their local public health authority or medical director who are in the chain of command with the HHS and CDC. Anything contrary to the standard messaging advocated by these "authorities" will be either rejected for release or edited for compliance. Recall the airline CEO's who were releasing statements regarding their support of vaccine mandates for their employees before the Supreme Court ruled against the utilization of OSHA public safety to enforce this. These corporations in the airlines industry crafted their press releases to the media in total allegiance to CDC and HHS mandate compliance. Big corporations all played along with the mainstream COVID narratives as they have also willingly accommodated other cancel culture and woke ideology propaganda. Added to the fact that public information has become a highly politicized tool in the hands of news media bureaucrats, it has been weaponized against conservatives.

No other time in American history have we witnessed such an outright assault on our freedom of speech as during the COVID pandemic. Social media giants enforced gestapo like tactics against those who dared to challenge the mainstream narratives supporting COVID vaccines and mask mandates. Facebook "police" deployed armies of "fact-checkers" who were quick to call out anything from alternative medical treatments for COVID to information about masks that disagreed with HHS and CDC approved guidelines. Fauci and the media tyrants were the only ones permitted to drive the narrative on COVID. Conservatives who voiced their opinion had their accounts on Twitter and YouTube cancelled. The "cancel culture" movement was empowered through mainstream media and social media platforms during the pandemic. This was not only true for dissenting "contrarians" who challenged popular mainstream narratives on COVID mandates, but it also impacted those in the scientific community and in medical professions who dared to disagree with the conventional status quo dialogue. This applied to anyone who supported anything other than a zoonotic origins theory of the virus. Anyone who claimed that COVID resulted from a lab leak or was a product of genetic engineering, were immediately branded as "conspiracy theorists." According to Markson, Facebook declared that after consulting with the WHO, it would remove any posts that said the virus was "man-made or had been bioengineered as a bioweapon."[180] Twitter and other social media companies made similar pledges to remove accounts that they claimed were spreading "misinformation." This comes as no surprise since media Giants like Google have been funding EcoHealth Alliance since 2010 in their early days of GOFR project collaboration with Wuhan.

Kennedy mentions that "Google has a long history of suppressing information that challenges vaccine industry profits" since their parent

---

[180] Markson, *What Really Happened in Wuhan*, 284-285.

company "Alphabet" owns several vaccine companies and has lucrative partnerships with vaccine manufacturers.[181] Other big tech social media platforms such as Pinterest, Instagram, and MailChimp began "scrubbing" information that was contrary to CDC guidance. Shortly after a physician by the name of Dr. Raoult questioned Fauci regarding the use of hydroxychloroquine (HCD) in a March 2020 news conference, Fauci's allies with the New York Times launched a campaign to discredit the doctor. Fauci has worked with Gates and Zuckerberg to censor his critics. We previously mentioned media elite's Jeff Bezos who uses his news company the Washington Post as a regular supporter of the mainstream narrative endorsed by the CDC and WHO. Bill Gates also funded his fact-checking organization, Politifact to suppress any reports on social media about COVID vaccine reactions and deaths. This organization also receives funding from the Robert Wood Johnson Foundation whose CEO Richard Besser who was formerly with the CDC owns $1.8 billion in Johnson & Johnson vaccine pharmaceutical stocks which has an active campaign to suppress information contrary to CDC narratives.[182] Mainstream media is quite selective of who they favorably endorse as "official spokespersons" – the ones who will agree with their liberal narratives. One such individual is Dr. Tara Kirk who is a senior scholar at the Bloomberg School of Health at Johns Hopkins University. Kirk works in the role of "Infodemiology" in which she serves as a media consultant and advisor to the U.S. government and WHO for "tracking the spread of misinformation (dissenting opinions) and curtailing its spread through risk communication and censorship."[183] She uses the standard terminology from government CERC/PIO planning methodology – "risk communication." Kirk is passionate about her role as a purveyor of the CDC/WHO narrative and is adamant about controlling what she labels as false and misleading information: "Unrest, due to false rumors and divisive

---

[181] Kennedy, *The Real Anthony Fauci*, 93-94

[182] Ibid, 180-181.

[183] Kennedy, *The Real Anthony Fauci*, 880-881.

messaging, is rising and is exacerbating spread of the disease as levels of trust fall and people stop operating with response efforts. This is a massive problem and threatens governments and trusted institutions." Even the CIA is calling for tighter media controls. Former CIA Deputy Director Arvil Haines issued warnings about "false information that hampers the government's ability to address the pandemic." On April 11, 2021, President Biden appointed Haines as the director of National Intelligence and is one of the highest officials in charge of pandemic response at the federal level.

On the international level there are prominent media czars such as Jane Halton who served as the finance and health minister in Australia and the former president of WHO's Health Assembly. Australia is a country which has gone to extreme governmental control measures to ensure pandemic compliance to include detention facilities for the unvaccinated. Halton also occupies a member the Executive Board of the Australian National COVID-19 Coordination Commission. For this commission she has authored guidelines for the government to implement a policy dictating that those who did not receive a vaccine would not be paid by their employers. Halton also was a consultant for the Gates Foundation in previous exercise simulations and proposed that data algorithms be created for the purpose of "sifting through information on social media platforms to protect the public from dangerous thoughts and information."[184] Another international media consultant is Chen Huang is an Apple research scientist and a Google expert who specializes in tracking and tracing individuals through facial recognition technology. Huang also in a pandemic simulation exercise sponsored by Gates recommended that "Twitter and Facebook delete accounts in order to prevent the spread of misinformation on COVID." On par with the CIA in the U.S. is the MI6 British spy agency that is also taking an active role in surveillance of individuals who questioned mainstream narratives on COVID by launching an "offensive cyber-operation to

---

[184] Ibid, 881.

disrupt anti-vaccine propaganda. MI6 spy Christopher Steele leads an organization called "Independent SAGE" made up of a highly influential group of social scientists, psychologists and media professionals who "use the news media to advocate for Zero COVID campaigns."

Media elites occupy positions of power and influence in the control and censorship of information. They have been a collective force against our constitutional republic and have trampled our freedom of speech and they have armed themselves through the COVID pandemic by setting themselves up for globalist domination in the new world order. In July 2021 there was an exclusive gathering of these billionaire elites Sun Valley, Idaho at an event called "Mogul Fest."[185] This event was attended by such power brokers in the media world such as Bill Gates (Microsoft), Mark Zuckerberg (Facebook), Jeff Bezos (Amazon), Mike Bloomberg, Larry Price (Google), Warren Buffet, Netflix CEO Reed Hastings, Disney CEO Robert Iger, and CNN's Anderson Cooper to name a few. According to Kennedy the collective net worth represented by these elites was over $3.8 trillion and their stated mission was firmly established: "Their censorship allowed their allies in the technocracy to effect the most extraordinary curtailment of American constitutional rights in history."[186] A media that is subservient to the government along with its constant barrage of censorship was far removed from the vision of our nation's founding fathers. Today's media elites and mainstream news resemble an Orwellian vision of Big Brother's state-controlled media:

> The Ministry of Truth — Minitrue, in Newspeak*
> (*Newspeak was the official language of Oceania.*) — was
> startingly different from any other object in site. It was

---

[185] Business Insider India, August 20, 2017. *Millionaires, Billionaires, Swarm to Sun Valley, Idaho for Allen & Company's Mogul Fest.* https://www.businessinsider.in/thelife/millionaires-billionaires-and-hangers-on-all-gather-in-sun-valley-idaho -for-allen-co-s-mogul-fest/slidelist/21056877.cms

[186] Kennedy, *The Real Anthony Fauci*, 892.

an enormous pyramidial structure of glittering white concrete, soaring up, terrace after terrace, three hundred meters into the air. From where Winston stood it was just possible to read, picked out on its white face in elegant lettering, the three slogans of the Party:

WAR IS PEACE

FREEDOM IS SLAVERY

IGNORANCE IS STRENGTH187

---

[187] George Orwell, *1984* (New York, NY: Signet Classics, 1949; reprint 1977), 4.

Chapter 7

Conclusion:
Where Do We Go From Here?

The web of subversion is not primarily a domestic growth. It is the domestic extension of an international organism. The spinning of the web and the defense against it are campaigns in a vast and continuing struggle that will decide what kind of world mankind is to live in. There is no easy and quick solution. To win we must also resolve to endure. We must have the will to survive and to be free. – James Burnham

The hypothesis set forth in this book is that the SARS-CoV-2 (COVID-19) virus was genetically engineered in a lab rather than being derived from a zoonotic origin (from animals). My belief is that the virus was created through gain of function research (GOFR) for nefarious purposes against nations and governments to undermine individual freedom and liberty. Furthermore, I maintain that SARS-CoV-2 is a bioweapon whether it was intentionally deployed or accidentally released. The release of this virus created the grand opportunity for the promotion of a globalist anti-nationalist agenda of an international reset. This global pandemic reset agenda constitutes an assault upon our American freedom and liberty and is a threat to our constitutional republic. Furthermore, the COVID-19 pandemic has become a highly politicized weapon in the hands of the socialist democratic left. This is evidenced with the government's overreach through draconian lockdowns, social-distancing, masking, and vaccine mandates. The cancel-culture movement, social justice riot violence through BLM and Antifa, media censorship, the propagation of divisive Critical Race Theory (CRT), and the weaponization of the FBI and DOJ against conservative citizens are all manifestations of this global reset agenda that have been launched in the aftermath of the COVID-19 pandemic. Feeling overwhelmed like the shell-shocked survivors of an apocalyptic plague most of us look at these events in our nation and around the world with a sense of disillusionment and wonder of what can be done to save our Republic. Our nation's early patriots also courageously faced overwhelming odds. In the battle at Lexington on April 19, 1775, a mere seventy-five minutemen militia soldiers stared down the rifle barrows of nearly 700 British infantry forces. Outgunned and outnumbered these valiant patriots stood their ground during tremendous opposition. Regarding the bravery of these soldiers, author Rick Green commented on the shot that was heard around the world at Lexington "The minutemen lit the torch of freedom and passed it to the next generation, and for over two centuries, Americans have willingly accepted that torch and preserved it for posterity. Now, it is our turn! This is our hour to stand guard at the watchtower of freedom. If that Torch of Freedom is to survive and be handed down from our generation to our children and grandchildren, then it has to begin here!"[188] Taking action to confront the COVID pandemic tyranny of our day will not be an easy task; it will require courage to face the opposition. It is as Burnham stated in our introduction quote: "There is no quick and easy solution. To win we must also resolve to endure. We must have the will to survive and to be free."[189] This "resolve to endure and the will to survive and to be free" must begin with us who love our nation and our constitution. In this final chapter I want to outline a course of action for us to ensure that we pass the "torch of freedom" to the next generation.

---

[188] Rick Green, *Freedom's Frame* (Dripping Springs, TX: Revolutionary Strategies, 2018), 183-184.

[189] Burnham, *The Web of Subversion*, 203.

U.S. Senate Legislation & House/Senate Bills

It is important to be aware of U.S. Senators who are taking an active voice in opposing the COVID pandemic tyranny and to support their efforts in addition to proposed House and Senate Bills. An important bill that you want to contact your district senate representative in your state to support is HR 4071 titled the Foreign Gain of Function Research Prevention Act of 2021.[190] This bill was initially sponsored by Rep. Brad Wenstrup (R-OH) who is also a physician. In the bill it aims "to prohibit the use of Federal funds to conduct or support certain gain-of-function research by a foreign adversary." Listed are such countries that are known adversarial foes of the U.S. such as China, Russia, Iran, and North Korea. This comes on the back end of the horrendous incidents where our tax-payer dollars went to fund the Wuhan research lab where the COVID virus was created. A senate bill that complements HR4071 is S.3159 titled "Fairness and Accountability in Underwriting Chinese Institutions Act. This senate legislation seeks to restrict the use of Federal Funds for gain-of-function research in the People's Republic of China and the People's Liberation Army as well as to demand accountability and transparency from the NIH and the HHS. The sponsor of this senate bill is Senator Joni Ernst of Iowa. In addition to these bills a key Congressional Act has been set forth by Senator Chris Stewart (R-UT). Stewart's act introduced in the Senate on November 16, 2021, is titled the "Fauci Act."[191] This legislation aims to ban U.S. funding for gain-of-function research in China and to produce a full accounting of U.S. tax dollars spent and restrict government officials who intentionally mislead Congress. The legislation bears the name of "Fauci" who was behind the GOFR projects being coordinated with China and includes a statement in the press release from Senator Joni Ernst: "While American tax dollars were being funneled

---

[190] Congres.Gov Site–https://www.congress.gov/bill/117th-congress/house-bill/4071

[191] Chris Stewart, U.S. Congressman. https://stewart.house.gov/news news/documentsingle.aspx?DocumentID=883

into Communist China to support dangerous experiments on coronaviruses at the Wuhan Lab, the head of the division funding those activities, Dr. Fauci, failed to tell the truth to Congress and to the American People about how our money was being spent." Rep. Stewart and Sen. Ernst have driven the momentum behind these efforts to get answers from the NIH about U.S. funding for dangerous experiments in China. The Fauci Act will be a key step toward holding China accountable and to demand transparency for ensuring justice. In addition to this act an important amendment called the "Reschenthaler Amendment" was voted for in the House of Representatives on September 23, 2021 calling for the prohibition of federal funding to EcoHealth Alliance. We mentioned Congressman Reschenthaler in Chapter four in our discussion of various GOFR/WIV funding sources. Reschenthaler regarding the amendment stated: "It is deeply disturbing that EcoHealth Alliance funneled American taxpayer dollars to support dangerous and potentially deadly research at the WIV, a laboratory run by the Chinese Communist Party (CCP) and tied to military biological research and the probable origin of the COVID-19 pandemic."[192]

---

[192] Guy Reschenthaler, U.S. Senator for Pennsylvania. September 23, 2021 Press Release *House Passes Reschenthaler Amendment Defunding EcoHealth Alliance*. https://reschenthaler .house.gov.

Senator Rand Paul of Kentucky, who is also a physician, is another vocal opponent of gain of function research is supporting legislation to repeal DC vaccine mandates for consumers and students. Paul who is known for his direct confrontations with Fauci, stated: "Enacting a vaccine mandate that infringes upon the right of parents to make medical decisions for their children and the personal liberties of consumers, in the capital of what is supposed to be the freest country in the world, doesn't sound like freedom at all. My legislation would stop these ridiculous, unscientific mandates and restore individual parental rights in the District."[193] Along with Paul an active challenger of the FDA regarding COVID treatment therapies is Senator Tom Cotton of Arkansas. In January of 2022, Cotton addressed the FDA's rationing of monoclonal antibody treatment based on race.[194] This is a key consideration for the rights of Americans seeking antibody treatment rather than the FDA mainline pharmaceuticals which are costly and are not effective. Cotton is known for being one of the first U.S. senators to publicly raise the possibility that the virus did not have a zoonotic origin and called out the GOFR projects on Coronavirus pathogens being researched in Wuhan. For this Cotton was attacked by all the media outlets as a conspiracist.[195] Another representative who is active in promoting legislation against COVID vaccine mandates is Senator Rick Scott of Florida. On February 3, 2022, Scott introduced the *OSHA Emergency Temporary Standard Clarification Act* which prevented the use of federal OSHA regulations for the enforcement of vaccine mandates in private business.[196] This legislation promoted by Sen. Scott along with Rand Paul and Marco Rubio prevents further unlawful, sweeping mandates by clarifying OSHA's role. Senator Marco Rubio also of Florida is challenging government's push back on granting religious

---

[193] Rand Paul, U.S. Senator for Kentucky. https://www.paul.senate.gov/

[194] Tom Cotton, U.S. Senator for Arkansas. https://www.cotton.senate.gov/

[195] Markson, *What Really Happened in Wuhan*, 69.

[196] Rick Scott, U.S. Senator for Florida. https://www.rickscott.senate.gov.

vaccine exemptions. A database known as the "Employee Religious Exception Request Information System that tracks names, religious beliefs and other private information of federal employees who have requested a religious exemption from the Biden Administration's COVID-19 vaccine mandate for all those working in federal positions of employment. This tracking database created watchlists through the DOJ and Homeland Security of all "non-vaccinated" federal employees requesting religious exemptions.[197] Therefore, Rubio and other bicameral lawmakers challenged the watchlist database under the provisions of U.S. Code 551; section 553 and are seeking legislative action as well. Sign up to receive updates on the above-mentioned bills and call the senate representatives in your state to let them know your support for this legislation. Also, when you vote in your local, state, and national elections, make sure that you research the candidates that are running and ask the essential questions: (1) Where do they stand on mandates for masks and vaccines? (2) Do they actively oppose gain-of-function research? (3) Do they have any vested interests in big pharma (i.e., investment portfolios, etc.)? and (4) What is their stand on quarantine and closures on businesses, schools, and churches? It is essential that American voters become informed if we are to protect our rights, liberties, and individual freedoms in the face of pandemic government overreach.

Supporting Brave Scientists and Medical Professionals Who Speak Out

The scientific community that bravely challenged the zoonotic origins theory risked public ridicule, were excommunicated from mainline scientific journals, and even worse had their research funding cancelled. Many of them remained silent until Sheri Markson conducted an interview with Dr. Nikolai Petrovsky Australia's Sky News Network regarding

---

[197] Marco Rubio, U.S. Senator for Florida. https://www.rubio.senate.gov/public/

his research that revealed the unique genetic properties of the COVID virus. Markson said that shortly after the interview Petrovsky "unexpectedly found himself at the center of global discussion as scientists who had come to similar conclusions about the virus...Many shared their own findings about suspicious features of the SARS-CoV-2 virus they'd been apprehensive about publicizing."[198] Markson says that it was soon after this that scientists who were not afraid to speak the truth about the fact that the virus was created in a lab and to challenge the mainline narratives came forward. We need to acknowledge and to show support for work and dedication of these scientists and to read about their research findings: Professor Richard Ebright from Rutgers University, U.S. virologist David Baltimore, American physicist Richard Muller, University of Hamburg's Dr. Roland Wiesendanger, Israeli geneticist Dr. Ronen Shemesh, Norwegian virologist Birger Sorensen, Dr. Steven Quay of Atossa Therapeutics, genetics researcher Yuri Deigin of Toronto, microbiologist Rossana Sergreto of Austria, and Professor David Relman of Harvard University are among these courageous scientists. Not only would I encourage you to enter their names into your search browser and download their research articles but also consider donating to their research projects. Some of these brave scientists have risked their funding and their reputation in the mainstream scientific community, but your support can help them. As we support those in the scientific community who are speaking the truth, many more scientists are bravely coming forward.

Another significant voice against the COVID-19 tyranny is attorney and public activist Robert F. Kennedy Jr. who is the nephew of the late President John F. Kennedy. In this book I quote Kennedy's book *The Real Anthony Fauci: Bill Gates, Big Pharma, and the Global War on Democracy and Public Health* which is an excellent resource. Kennedy has been labeled as a conspiracy theory extremist especially since he has become a vocal challenger of the COVID vaccines. There is a push

---

[198] Markson, *What Really Happened in Wuhan*, 165-190.

to have children under the age of five vaccinated for COVID under the Emergency Use Authorization (EUA). This EUA permitted the FDA approval for big pharma companies such as Pfizer, Moderna, and Johnson & Johnson to vaccinate young children. Kennedy's work through his *Children's Health Defense* that was established in 2011 has come to the forefront by legally challenging the EUA used by big pharma.[199] Kennedy who is a supporter of physicians who are speaking the truth on masks and COVID vaccines and lists this information as well as legal resources on his web site at childrenshealthdefense.org. Some of the physicians that are speaking the truth about alternative effective treatments for COVID as well as the science behind everything from masking to vaccines have been listed by Kennedy[200]: epidemiologist Dr. Harvey Risch of Yale University, Dr. Robert Malone the original inventor of the mRNA vaccine technologies, Dr. Geert Vanden Bossche with Global Alliance for Vaccines & Immunization, Dr. Michael Yeadon, respiratory pharmacologist, Dr. Luc Montagnier, Nobel Prize Virologist, Dr. Wolfgang Wodarg, pulmonologist, Dr. Peter McCullough, Chief of Internal Medicine at Baylor Medical who has been featured in extensive videos and podcasts, Dr. Peter Doshi, Associate Editor at the British Medical Journal, Dr. Paul E. Marik, Founder of Front-Line Covid-19 Critical Care Alliance, Dr. Peirre Kory, President & Chief Medical Officer of Frontline Covid-19 Critical Care Alliance, Dr. Byram Bridle, Viral Immunology Professor, Dr. Tess Lawrie, M.D., Dr. Didier Raoult, microbiologist, Dr. Peter Breggin, psychiatrist, Dr. Meryl Nass, toxicologist, Dr. Vladimir Zelnko, M.D., Dr. Charles Hoffe, M.D., Dr. James Todaro, M.D., Dr. Scott Jensen, Medical Professor, Dr. Ryan Cole, pathologist, Dr. Jacob Puliyel, Pediatrics, Dr. Christine Northrup, OB-GYN professor, Dr. Richard Urso, Oncologist, Dr. Joseph Ladapo, Florida Surgeon General, Dr. Martin Kulldorff, Harvard Professor of Medicine, Dr. Michael Levitt, Stanford University biophysicist, Dr. Satoshi Omura, Nobel Prize biochemist, Dr. Paul E. Alexander,

---

[199] Children's Health Defense: https://childrenshealthdefense.org

[200] Kennedy, *The Real Anthony Fauci*, 10-14.

M.D., Dr. Clare Craig, UK pathologist, Dr. Lee Merritt, U.S. Navy Physician, Dr. Sucharit Bhakdi, microbiologist, Dr. Jay Bhattacharya, professor of medicine at Stanford University, Dr. David Katz, Yale research physician, Dr. John Ioannidis, Stanford University, Dr. Sunetra Gupta, Oxford University epidemiologist, Dr. Catherine L. Lawson, professor Rutgers, Dr. Salmaan Keshavjee, medical professor Harvard, Dr. Laura Lazzeroni, biomedical data Stanford, Dr. Cody Meissner, pediatrics professor, Dr. Lisa White, epidemiology Oxford, Dr. Ariel Munitz, microbiologist Tel Aviv University, Dr. Motti Gerlic, microbiologist Tel Aviv University, Dr. Angus Dalgleish, professor of infectious disease London University, Dr. Helen Colhoun, medical informatics University of Edinburg, Dr. Simon Thornley, biostatistician, and Dr. Stephanie Seneff, MIT. This is a valuable list of distinguished medical professionals who represent a variety of fields in epidemiology, vaccine science pharmacology, pulmonology, internal medicine, microbiology, biochemistry, pediatrics, oncology, and pathology. You can take advantage of their knowledge by entering their names into your search browser. Kennedy aptly introduces these medical professionals as a "symbol of clarity and truth who resist the rising medical authoritarianism."

Holding "Socialistic" Public Health Agencies Accountable

The Bill and Melinda Gates Foundation have the title banner on their website which sounds like an idealist's dream for achieving humanitarian global utopia: *We are a nonprofit fighting poverty, disease, and inequity around the world.* The term "inequity" is broadly defined as an "injustice or unfairness" and is also called "health disparities." The counter-term to health inequities or health disparities is "health equity" and is a code word propagated extensively in the annals of public health socialism. This term is further explained by the Democratic Socialists of America (DSA): "Health disparities are not just a biological reality; they are a form of social inequality because they are structured according to unjust power arrangements. Social stratification drives group disparities in health, so health status reflects social status. Public health advocates use of the term "health inequities" to describe these differences in health because they result from the systemic, unjust, and avoidable distribution of social, economic, political, and environmental resources needed for health and well-being."[201] Notice key terms that are being used here: "unjust power arrangements, distribution of resources, group disparities" are all consistent with a Marxist ideology. The Democratic Socialist description of health inequities resembles something right out of *The Communist Manifesto*: "This school of Socialism dissected with great acuteness the contradictions in the conditions of modern (*capitalist*) systems...the inevitable ruin of the petty bourgeois and peasant, the misery of the proletariat, the anarchy in production, **the crying inequalities in the distribution of wealth**."[202] The DSA further explains that these public health inequities (inequalities) are caused by systemic racism in America fueled by white supremacy on health: "institutionalized racism produces unequal health outcomes that cannot be corrected by access to health care alone."

[201] Kate Arnoff, Peter Dreier & Michael Kazin, editors, *We Own the Future: Democratic Socialism – American Style* (New York, NY: The New Press, 2021), 228.

[202] Karl Marx, *The Communist Manifesto* (Germany: Sanage Publishing, 1848), 53.

The campaign for socialist public health equities is not only the theme of the Gates Foundation but is also a sentiment echoed throughout many of the federal institutions of public health. The CDC has the topic of health equity listed under their National Center for Chronic Disease Prevention and Health Promotion (NCCDPHP): "Health equity is achieved when every person has the opportunity to attain his or her full health potential and no one is disadvantaged from achieving this potential because of social position or other socially determined circumstances."[203] The NIH also follows with their platform called "Health Equity Research" under their banner *Ending Structural Racism* (another term for systemic racism).[204] Their agenda to remove barriers to advancing health disparities research is explained: "Research on health disparities examines the influence of environment, social determinants, and other underlying mechanisms leading to differences in health outcomes." The Federal Health and Human Services also targets health disparities as "nondiscriminatory quality healthcare services" under content created by the Office of Civil Rights.[205] All of these public health agencies within the domain of CDC, NIH, and HHS all share funding and distribute funding to state and local health departments around the nation. Not all aspects of public health services are bad — restaurant food inspections, sanitation, clean water, communicable disease epidemiology, etc. provide a reasonable level of service for communities. However, to an extent local public health programs have also become politicized during the COVID pandemic. I was not aware of this until just before I retired from my career field. Our unit was asked to assist with planning and logistics for COVID vaccine operations in the latter part of 2020. At that

[203] Centers for Disease Control & Prevention: National Center for Chronic Disease Prevention & Health Promotion — Health Equity. https://www.cdc.gov/chronic-disease/healthequity/index.htm

[204] National Institutes of Health — *Ending Structural Racism*. https://www.nih.gov/ending-structural-racism/health-equity-research.

[205] HHS Civil Rights — *Health Disparities*. https://www.hhs.gov/civil-rights/for-individuals/special-topics/health-disparities/index.html

time, I had very little knowledge regarding the problems with mRNA vaccine technology, but we were told by state and federal public health agencies that vaccines would be fully approved through emergency use authorization (EUA) by the FDA. Knowing that historically vaccines such as for smallpox, measles, etc. were developed over years of clinical testing to determine their efficacy and safety, a government mandated approval within a matter of a few months was highly questionable.

However, way before any approvals for the vaccines had been discussed there was planning already underway months in advance for vaccine deployment strategies. When I was involved with logistics planning conference calls, I was surprised to find two personnel with considerable influence that were assigned to make ready for the deployment of vaccines: the public health equities manager and the public information manager (in charge of news media). The health equities section worked closely with the public information office to ensure that minority populations and faith-based organizations (FBO's) had targeted messaging, social media, news media, advertising, and town hall meetings so that they would be educated on the "urgency of getting a COVID vaccine". Furthermore, they were to identify leaders in the minority communities (African American, Hispanic, Asian, etc.) and leaders in churches, synagogues, and mosques who would encourage their respective communities to "get the jab." I have had enough direct experience with COVID vaccine planning logistics during 2020 through 2021 in conference calls regarding public health information campaigns on social distancing, masking, and "pandemic public safety" to tell you that it is well funded in local health departments and is a "well-tuned propaganda machine" that also serves the interests of federal public health agencies.

The agenda of CDC, NIH and HHS have been active in contributing to GOFR projects, enforcement of closures, mask and vaccine mandates and have leveraged the public health departments at the state and local level to do their bidding. Especially with the socialist construct of public health equities, local health departments have been liberally funded to support COVID programs in your neighborhood to include everything from contact tracing, testing, vaccinations, and quarantine enforcement. Funding is also provided to public health information officers for COVID related messaging, advertising, and social media campaigns promoting masking and vaccines. An association known as the National Association of County and City Health Officials (NACCHO) is an organization headquartered in Washington, D.C. that is a network for local city, county, metropolitan, and district health departments provides guidance for public health infrastructure to include pandemic preparedness, climate change planning, and health equity programs. Most local health departments have a fully funded health equities program that is closely integrated with all other public health programs. These programs must be properly vetted through the public health equities to ensure compliance with "socialized public health." If you go online to check out your local health department, it will provide you with details on how they are staffed and maintained with either a health equities director or manager and depending upon the size of your jurisdiction, there might be multiple staff who oversee operations in your neighborhood for health disparities agendas.

While each state varies in terms of how their local health departments are organized – for instance some are entirely run by the state health department or the state health commissioner while other states will have both state, county, and city run health departments. Nearly all local health departments have a public health authority and/or a public health director who assumes the role of an acting authority to implement and to enforce public health measures. These measures can include the enforcement of isolation and quarantine measures, business and school closures, and vaccine operations. Local health authorities and their directors have considerable legal domain to exercise influence over their jurisdictions. Depending upon how your state government is set up with a central state health commissioner or a central public health department, there are laws at the state level for health and human services that yield considerable power and influence. The state health commissioners work closely with CDC quarantine officers and through the state health and human services code of law can have the power to implement isolation and quarantine protocols. These measures can either be used to arrest and quarantine individuals or to even lock down entire institutions to include churches, businesses, and schools. The response plans for isolation and quarantine enforcement are called "non-pharmaceutical interventions" (NPI) and are included in nearly every written situation manual used for public health regional and local exercises and simulations (recall in the previous chapter how the federal agencies HHS, CDC, & NIH along with the Gates Foundation conducted pandemic exercises). Local health departments are required to conduct on a regular basis: pandemic exercises, mass fatality exercises, isolation, and quarantine exercises to receive their funding. Most public health emergency preparedness programs (PHEP) receive millions of dollars of funding annually to ensure that they train and exercise their personnel in these preparedness "target capabilities." These programs also include planning for what is called "mass prophylaxis" for deployment and dispensing of COVID vaccines in large populations. Most of these programs are part of the older bioterrorism preparedness programs such as the Strategic National Stockpile (SNS) which stockpiled vaccines and medical countermeasures for everything from bioterrorism attacks to pandemics.

Here's a simple three-step action plan for "holding public health" accountable in your state, county, or city:

1. Determine if your local city or county health department has a health authority or a director. Find out who this individual is accountable to. Do they report to a county judge, city mayor or state health commissioner? The elected officials must oversee public health operations and planning within a framework of transparency – this will include city council meetings run by the mayor or county commissioner courts that are run by the judge. Go to the meeting agendas online for your city or county and review the public health dockets. These review all planning and funding sessions for your local health department.

2. Budgets for the local and state health departments are available to the public. Review your local health department budgets. How much is being allocated for "public health equities" or COVID vaccine operations? What about pandemic planning, training, and exercises? You will be surprised to see how much federal funding from the CDC and HHS are going to support COVID programs at the local level. Call or write your mayor, judge, or state governor's office to hold these elected officials accountable for the funding and support of these COVID programs.

3. Go to "town-hall" meetings and get to know your elected officials to include your local health department authority and/or director. Find out where they stand on mask and vaccine mandates. Unfortunately, most of the health departments follow the "party-line" from the CDC and HHS where they get their funding from. However, you can put pressure on your local and state elected officials to keep these public health authorities in check.

Concluding Thoughts

The COVID pandemic has impacted us with the loss of life, jobless-ness, and some of our basic rights and freedoms in our constitutional republic. It has disrupted life in every area imagined nationally and globally. We will eventually return to a "back to normal" (although the mainstream narrative maintains that there will never be a normal but only a "new normal"). As we put the pieces back together again, it is important we review the lessons learned with the COVID upset in this generation. We must realize that it is not the government's role to mandate any health and medical requirements. American citizens have the right to choose for themselves whether to get a vaccine or to wear a mask. If our personal choices do not violate ethical, moral and spiritual law, or harm others, we have the right to choose for ourselves. We have the right to listen to all the opinions of the scientific and med-ical community and not only those that are dictated by mainstream narratives endorsed in the media. The American people deserve to hear the full story on vaccine safety and the science behind masking and social distancing. There needs to be due process in the develop-ment of any vaccine to ensure its safety and efficacy. We do not need to be railroaded by any medications delivered by big pharma before they are safely vetted through a rigorous clinical trial process, not by hasty and dangerous federal EUA's that are driven by political agendas. Big government and globalism seek to impose control (revolution) over the people through crisis. This time the crisis was a COVID pan-demic that was engineered in a lab as a bioweapon against humanity to disrupt nations and to attempt to assert itself through a global reset. This manifested with business, school and church closures and man-dates for masks, social distancing, and vaccines. The next national or global crisis may or may not be a pandemic. The plan for global reset will always attempt to use some sort of health, economic, or natural disaster as a crisis. This plan for global tyranny that suppresses indi-vidual rights and religious freedoms of individuals and nations is as old as "ancient Babylon" and is a force to be reckoned with in each tyrant from Hitler, Mussolini, Stalin, and Mao that attempts to subvert our God given rights. We must be all the wiser and cherish the heritage of our nation and its founding fathers. We can learn from their struggles as they faced ruthless tyranny when they drafted our Declaration of Independence and our Constitution. For our generation they serve as examples to those of us who are willing to stand for freedom. It is as Rick Green said of these brave patriots who have gone on before us: "There has always been a remnant of heroes willing to sacrifice their lives, fortunes, and sacred honor to protect the torch of freedom."[206] We are also grateful for our modern day heroes who are the "resistance force" in the face of this pandemic and the patriots who rise to the occasion to challenge mainstream media, censorship, and tyrannical government control. Alongside of them let us never tire of "fighting the good fight."

---

[206] Rick Green, *Chasing American Legends: Pursuing Truth About History's Heroes* (Dripping Springs, TX: Patriot Academy, 2018), 131.

BIBLIOGRAPHIC
LISTING OF SOURCES

BOOKS

Abultalem, Yasmeen & Paletta, Damian. *Nightmare Scenario: Inside the Trump Administration's Response to the Pandemic that Changed the World.* New York, NY: Harper-Collins, 2021.

Alibek, Ken with Handelman, Stephen. *Biohazard: The Chilling True Story of the Largest Covert Biological Weapons Program in the World – Told from the Inside by the Man Who Ran It.* New York, NY: Dell Publishing, 1999.

Arnoff, Kate, Dreier, Peter & Kazin, Michael editors. *We Own the Future: Democratic Socialism – American Style.* New York, NY: The New Press, 2021.

Beck, Glenn. *Crimes or Cover Up?* PDF copy. November 2021.

Burnham, James. *The Web of Subversion.* Belmont, MA: Americanist Library, 1954.

Couch, Dick, *The U.S. Armed Forces Nuclear, Biological, & Chemical Survival Manual: Everything You Need to Know to Protect Yourself*

& Your Family from the Growing Terrorist Threat. New York, NY: Perseus Books, 2003.

Garcia, Antonio F., Rand, Dan, & Rinard, John Howard, Jr., editors. *Jane's Chemical, Biological, Radiological, & Nuclear (CBRN) Response Handbook*, 4th, ed. United Kingdom: IHS Sentinel House, 2011.

Green, Rick. *Chasing American Legends: Pursuing Truth About History's Heroes.* Dripping Springs, TX: Patriot Academy, 2018.

Green, Rick. *Freedom's Frame.* Dripping Springs, TX: Revolutionary Strategies, 2018.

Hamilton, Clive & Ohlberg, Mareike, *Hidden Hand: How the Chinese Communist Party is Reshaping the World*. London, England: One World Books, 2020.

Kennedy, Robert F. Jr. *The Real Anthony Fauci: Bill Gates, Big Pharma and the Global War on Democracy & Public Health.* New York, NY: Skyhorse Publishing, 2021.

Liang, Qiao and Xiangsui, Wang, *Un-Restricted Warfare; Translated from the Original People's Liberation Army Documents* Brattleboro, VT: Echo Point Books & Media, 1999

Levy, Barry S. & Sidel, Victor W. *Terrorism & Public Health: A Balanced Approach to Strengthening Systems and Protecting People*. New York, NY: Oxford University Press, 2003.

Markson, Sharri. *What Really Happened in Wuhan: A Virus Like No Other; Countless Infections, Millions of Deaths*. New York, NY: Harper Collins, 2021.

Marx, Carl. *The Communist Manifesto*. Germany: Sanage Publishing, 1848.

Orwell, George, *1984*. New York, NY: Signet Classics, 1949; reprint 1977.

O'Toole, Tara, Inglesby, Thomas V., & Henderson, Donald A. *Why Understanding Biological Weapons Matters to Medical & Public Health Professionals* compiled within *Bioterrorism Guidelines for Medical & Public Health Management*, New York, NY: The American Medical Association, 2001.

Peters, C.J. & Olshaker, Mark. *Virus Hunter: Thirty Years of Battling Hot Viruses Around the World*. New York, NY: Random House Anchor Books, 1997.

Pipes, Richard. *Communism: A History.* New York, NY: Random House, 2003.

Schwab, Klaus & Malleret, Thierry. *COVID-19: The Great Reset*, Geneva, Switzerland: Forum Publishing, 2020.

Schwartz, Peter. *Scenarios for the Future of Technology & International Development.* May 2010. The Rockefeller Foundation & Global Business Network.

Service, Robert. *Comrades: A History of World Communism*. Cambridge, MA: Harvard University Press, 2007.

Spalding, Robert. *Stealth War: How China Took Over While America's Elite Slept*. USA: Penguin Random House, 2019.

WEB SOURCES

Aryan, Javin. *A Look at China's Biowarfare Ambitions*, June 2, 2021, Observer Research Foundation. Source Accessed January 4, 2022 from https://www.orfonline.org/expert-speak/a-look-at-chinas-biowarfare-ambitions/

Bartow, Eleanor. *France Warned US in 2015 About China's Wuhan Lab, Investigator Says*, The Daily Signal, July 18, 2021. Source obtained November 9, 2021 from https://www.dailysignal.com/2021/07/28/ france-warned-us-in-2015-about-chinas-wuhan-lab-investigator-says/.

Basu, Mohana. *What is Gain of Function? Research Field Back in Focus as COVID Linked to China Lab Accident.* May 22, 2021. Source accessed July 6, 2021 from https://theprint.in/theprint-essential/what-is-gain-of-function-research-field-back-in-focus-as-covid-linked-to-china-lab-accident/662625/.

Biomedical Advanced Research Development Authority website: https://www.medicalcountermeasures.gov/BARDA.

Bill & Melinda Gates Foundation website: https://www.gatesfoundation.

Blinken, Antony J., *Trump is Ceding Global Leadership to China*, November 8, 2017. New York Times. https://www.nytimes.com/2017 /11/08/opinion/trump-china-xi-jinping.html?_r=0.

Business Insider India, August 20, 2017. *Millionaires, Billionaires, Swarm to Sun Valley, Idaho for Allen & Company's Mogul Fest.* https://www.businessinsider.in/thelife/

millionaires-billionaires-and-hangers-on-all-gather-in-sun-valley-idaho -for-allen-co-s-mogul-fest/slidelist/21056877.cms.

Carlson, Tucker. *Mark Milley Committed Treason, and Others Were Implicated*, Fox News, September 14, 2021. https://www.foxnews.com/ opinion/tucker-carlson-mark-milley-committed-treason.

Centers for Disease Control & Prevention: National Center for Chronic Disease Prevention & Health Promotion – Health Equity. https://www.cdc.gov/chronicdisease/healthequity/index.htm.

Children's Health Defense: https://childrenshealthdefense.org.

Cohen, Jan. *Wuhan Seafood Market May Not be Source of Novel Virus Spreading Globally: Description of Earliest Cases Suggests Outbreak Began Elsewhere.* January 26, 2020 Science Magazine. Source accessed October 15, 2021 from https://www.science.org/ content/article/ wuhan-seafood-market-may-not-be-source-novel-virus-spreading-globally.

Collins, Michael. *The WHO and China: Dereliction of Duty*, February 27, 2020. Asia Unbound, Council on Foreign Relations. Site accessed December 8, 2021 from https://www.cfr.org/blog/ who-and-china-dereliction-duty.

COVID-19 Virology, Biology & Novel Laboratory Diagnosis. Source accessed June 10, 2021, from https://www.ncib.nlm.nih.gov/pmc/ articles/PMC7883242.

Chen, Stephen. *The Chinese Book at the Bottom of the SARS Bioweapons Claims*, South China Morning Post, October 5, 2021. https://www.msn.com/en-xl/news/other/

the-chinese-book-at-the-bottom-of-the-sars-bioweapons-claims/
ar-BB1gzDAb.

Chellaney, Brahma. *The World Health Organization Must Stop Covering Up China's Mistakes*, April 23, 2020. *The Project Syndicate*. Source Accessed December 8, 2021 from https://www.marketwatch.com/story/ the-who-has-a-big-china-problem-2020-04-2.

China's Wuhan Institute of Virology, the Lab at the Core of the Coronavirus Controversy, source obtained November 9, 2021, from https://www.livemint.com/news/world/world/china-s-wuhan-institute-of-virology-the-lab-at-the-core-of-a-virus-controversy-11587266870143.html.

Congres.Gov Site—https://www.congress.gov/bill/117th-congress/house-bill/4071.

Tom Cotton, U.S. Senator for Arkansas. https://www.cotton.senate.gov/.

Defense Advanced Research Projects Agency (DARPA); COVID, March 19, 2021. Website: https://www.darpa. mil/work-with-us/covid-19.

Edelman, Adam. *Biden's Comments Downplaying China Threat to U.S. Fire Up Pols on Both Sides*, NBC News; May 2, 2019. https://www.nbcnews.com/politics /2020-election/biden-s-comments-downplaying-china-threat-u-s-fires-pols-n1001236.

Emerging Diseases from Animals, 2015 NIH article. Site accessed December 9, 2021 from https://www.ncbi.nlm.nih.gov/ pmc/articles/PMC7124125/

Fox News, November 4, 2021, *Rand Paul Accuses Fauci of Changing 'Gain-of-Function' Definition*, site accessed on December 16, 2021 from https://www.foxnews.com/politics/rand-paul-anthony-fauci -senate-hearing-gain-of-function.

Gertz, Bill. *China Deception Fuels Fear of Biological Weapons Ethnic Experiments*, The Washington Times, May 14, 2020. Source acquired November 8, 2021 at https://www.washingtontimes.com/news/2020/ may/14/ china-deception-fuels-fears-biological-weapons-eth/.

Grossman, Hannah. *Ted Cruz Shreds Fauci Delusions Over His I Represent Science Remark*. November 29, 2021. Source accessed January 19, 2022 from https://www.foxnews.com/media / ted-cruz-anthony-fauci-represent-science-remarks-most-danger- ous-bureaucrat

Guy Lorin Reschenthaler, 14th Congressional District. Press Release, May 14, 2021. *$1.1 Million in Taxpayer Funding Sent to the Wuhan Institute of Technology.* https://reschenthaler.house.gov/media/ press-releases/reschenthaler-uncovers-11-million-taxpayer-fund- ing-sent-wuhan-institute.

Healey, Isaac. *Bats and Pangolins Not Sold at Wuhan Markets Says Oxford Research*, The Oxford Student, June 8, 2021. Site accessed December 9, 2021 from https://www.oxfordstudent. com/2021/06/08/ bats-and-pangolins-not-sold-at-wuhan-markets- says-oxford-research.

Hounsell, Scott. *Wuhan Lab Funder Daszak Emailed Fauci, Thanking Him for Dismissing Lab Leak Theory*. Red State, June 1, 2021. Source accessed January 18, 2022 from https://redstate.com/scotthounsell/2021/06/01/

breaking-wuhan-lab-funder-email-thanks-fauci-for-running-defense-on-lab-leak-theory-n389836.

HHS Civil Rights – *Health Disparities*. https://www.hhs.gov/civil-rights/for-individuals/special-topics/health-disparities/index.html.

In-Q-Tel: *COVID-19 Efforts in B.Next*. Site: https://www. bnext.org.

Institute for Disease Modeling, Bill & Melinda Gates Foundation. https://www.gatesfoundation.org/our-work/programs/global-health/Institute-for-Disease-Modeling.

Kania, Elsa B. & Vorndick, Wilson. August 14, 2019, *Weaponizing Biotech: How China's Military is Preparing for a New Domain of Warfare*. Source accessed on October 25, 2021 from https://www.defenseone.com/ideas//2019/08/chinas-military-pursuing-biotech/159167/.

Kalmanson, Jennifer. *The Humanist*, October 12, 2021.Source accessed January 19, 2022, from https://thehumanist.com/magazine/fall-2021/features/2021-humanist-of-the-year-dr-anthony-s-fauci

Lohman, Walter & Rhee, Justin. *2021 China Transparency Report*, (Washington, DC: The Heritage Foundation, 2021), Preface.

Loro Horato. *China's Main Interests in Afghanistan are of a Strategic & Political Nature*, August 10, 2021, Defence Point. https://defence-point.com/2021/08/21/ china-s-main-interests-in-afghanistan-are-of-a-strategic-and-political-nature/.

Madhani, Aamer. ABC News, *Harris Tells UN Body It's Time to Prepare for the Next Pandemic.* April

26, 2021. https//abcnews.go.com/Politics/wireStory/
harris-body-time-prep-pandemic-77315989.

Mazumdaru, Srinivas. DW Asia April 17, 2020, *What
Influence Does China Have Over the WHO?*, Site accessed
December 8, 2021 from https://www.dw.com/en/
what-influence-does-china-have-over-the-who/a-53161220.

Massoglia, Anna. *Beijing Winter Olympic's Corporate Sponsors
are also Big Lobbying Spenders*, February 3, 2002. Open Secrets
– Following Money in Politics. https://www.opensecrets.org/
news/2022/02/beijing-winter-olympics-corporate-sponsors-are-al-
so-big-lobbying-spenders/.

Miller, Andrew Mark. *Fox News Special Report Outlines Fresh
Questions on What Fauci, Government Knew About COVID Origin*,
January 26, 2022. https://www.foxnews.com/politics/special-report-
outlines-fresh-questions-on-what-fauci-government-knew-about-
covid-origin.

NIH Director Announcement, *NIH Lifts Funding Pause on
Gain-of-Function Research*, December 19, 2017. Accessed
source on December 13, 2021 from https://www.nih.
gov/about-nih/who-we-are/nih-director/statements/
nih-lifts-funding-pause-gain-function-research.

NIH Director Press Release, *Testimony on the Transformative Power
of Biomedical Research*; Witness appearing before the House
Appropriations Subcommittee on Labor, HHS, Education, and
Related Agencies. May 17, 2017. Source Accessed on December
13, 2021 from https://www.nih.gov/about-nih /who-we-are/
nih-director/testimony-transformative-power-biomedical-research.

National Institutes of Health – *Ending Structural Racism*. https://www.nih.gov/ending-structural-racism/health-equity-research.

Pompeo, Michael R. at the Hudson Institute's Herman Kahn Award Gala, October 30, 2019. Site accessed January 13, 2022 from https://uy.usembassy.gov/michael-r-pompeo-at-the-hudson-institutes-herman-kahn-award-gala/

PREDICT Project Site, USAID. Source accessed on June 9, 2021 from https://ohi.vetmeducdavids.edu/programs- projects/predict-project.

Paul, Rand. U.S. Senator for Kentucky. https://www.paul.senate.gov/.

Reschenthaler, Guy. U.S. Senator for Pennsylvania. September 23, 2021 Press Release *House Passes Reschenthaler Amendment Defunding EcoHealth Alliance*. https://reschenthaler .house.gov.

Rubio, Marco. U.S. Senator for Florida. https://www.rubio.senate.gov/public/.

Schaeffer, Brett D. *The World Health Organization Bows to China*; Heritage Foundation Commentary Global Politics, April 28, 2020. Source accessed December 8, 2021 from https://www.heritage.org/global-politics/commentary / the-world-health-organization-bows-china.

Schwab, Klaus. "What is Stakeholder Capitalism?" *Global Agenda*. https://www.weforum.org/agenda/2021/01/klaus-schwab -on-what-is-stakeholder-capitalism-history-relevance/.

Scott, Rick. U.S. Senator for Florida. https://www.rickscott.senate.gov.

Stewart, Chris. U.S. Congressman. https://stewart.house.gov/news news/documentsingle.aspx?DocumentID=883.

USAID Press Release: *USAID Announces Robust Targets to Advance President Biden's Prepare Climate Initiative*, November 1, 2021. Source obtained November 10, 2021, from USAID site: https://www.usaid.gov/news-information/press-releases/nov-1-2021-us-aid-announces-robust-targets-advance-president-biden-prepare-climate-initiative.

Toosi, Nahal. *Pompeo Blasts China on Anniversary of Tiananmen Square Massacre*, June 3, 2019, Politico. Source accessed January 4, 2022 from https://www.politico. eu/article/pompeo-china-tiananmen-square-massacre/

Victor, Daniel, Myers, Steven Lee, & Blinder, Alan. *Pelosi Warns U.S. Athletes Not to Anger China's Government with Protests*, February 4, 2022. The New York Times.

World Economic Forum LLC, *About*. https://www.weforum.org/ / about/world-economic-forum-llc.

Wuhan Institute of Virology (cas.cn), accessed June 28, 2021, from http://english.whiov.cas.cn/.

GOVERNMENT PUBLICATIONS

Adherence to and Compliance with Arms Control, Nonproliferation, and Disarmament Agreements & Comments, published and prepared by the U.S. Department of State

Ainscough, Michael J. Col., USAF. *Next Generation Bioweapons: The Technology of Genetic Engineering Applied to Biowarfare &*

Bioterrorism. The Counterproliferation Papers Future Warfare Series No. 14. USAF Counterproliferation Center, Maxwell AFB, Alabama

Anthrax Investigation "Amerithrax" Federal Bureau of Investigation, https://www.fbi.gov/history /famous-cases/ amerithrax-or-anthrax-investigation.

Congressional Letter, February 7, 2022 to the Honorable Samantha Power regarding USAID funding to EcoHealth

Criminal & Epidemiological Investigation Handbook; 2011 edition: U.S. Department of Justice Federal Bureau of Investigation.

Framework for Guiding Funding Decisions about Proposed Research Involving Enhanced Potential Pandemic Pathogens, 2017 U.S. Department of Health & Human Services.

Homeland Security Presidential Directive (HSPD-21), George W. Bush authorized for press release on October 18, 2007. Source Acquired November 4, 2021 from https://irp.fas.org/ offdocs/nspd/ hspd-21.htm

Letter to the Honorable Lloyd J. Austin III and Gen. Mark A Milley; Congress of the U.S. House of Representatives, Mike Gallagher, June 21, 2021. Site accessed December 3, 2021 from https://galla-gher.house.gov/ sites/gallagher.house.gov/files/Letter_World%20 Military%20Games_6.21.pdf.

The Origins of COVID-19: An Investigation of the Wuhan Institute of Virology. August 2021. House Foreign Affairs Committee Report Minority Staff, Michael T. McCaul; One Hundred Seventeenth Congress.

Recommendations for the Evaluation and Oversight of Proposed Gain-of-Function Research, A Report of the National Science Advisory Board for Biosecurity, May 2016.

United Nations Office for Disarmament Affairs, https://www.un.org/disarmament/biological-weapons.

U.S. Embassy Tbilisi in Georgia. Site accessed June 21, 2021 at https://ge.usembassy.gov/fact-sheet-activity-at-the-wuhan-institute-of-virology/

USAMRIID's Medical Management of Biological Casualties Handbook, 6th edition, April 2005. Frederick MD – Ft. Detrick, 2005

JOURNALS & SCIENTIFIC RESEARCH ARTICLES

Carlos Farkas, Abstract: *Insights on Early Mutational Events in SARS-CoV-2 Virus Reveal Founder Effects Across Geographical Regions*, May 21, 2020. Source accessed on June 24, 2021 from https://peerj.com/articles/ articles/9255/#supplementary-material

Han Xia, Yi Huang, Haixia Ma, Bobo Liu, Weiwei Xie, Donglin Song, & Zhiming Yuan, Emerging Infectious Diseases Online Report; Vol. 25, No. 5. May 2019. *Biosafety Level 4 Laboratory User Training Program, China* Centers for Disease Control & Prevention. Accessed November 9, 2021 from https://wwwnc.cdc.gov/eid/article/25/5/18-0220_article.

Jacobsen, Rowan. *Inside the Risky Bat-Virus Engineering that Links America to Wuhan*, June 29, 2021, MIT Pandemic Technology Project. Source accessed October 15, 2021, from https://www.technologyreview.com/2021/06/29/1027290/gain-of-function-risky-bat-virus-engineering- links-america-to-wuhan/.

The Lancet, *Statement in Support of the Scientists, Public Health Professionals, and Medical Professionals of China Combatting COVID-19*. Volume 395; Issue 10226, E42-E43, March, 07, 2020. Source accessed January 18, 2022 from https://www.thelancet.com/ journals/lancet/article /PIIS0140-6736(20)30418-9/fulltext.

Monali C. Rahalkar and Rahul A. Bahulikar, *Letha Pneumonia Cases in Mojiang Miners (2012) and the Mineshaft Could Provide Important Clues to the Origin of SARS-CoV-2*, Frontiers in Public Health, October 20, 2020. Vol. 8; Article 581569.

National Institute of Allergy and Infectious Diseases, *SARS-CoV-2 and NIAID – supported Bat Coronavirus Research*, site accessed on December 16, 2021 from https://www.niaid.nih.gov/diseases conditions/coronavirus-bat-research.

Nature Medicine: Vol. 21, No. 12, December 2015, *A SARS-Like Cluster of Circulating Bat Coronaviruses Shows Potential for Human Emergence*, Nature America Inc.

Quay, Steven C., Rahalkar, Monali, Jones, Adrian & Bhulikar, Rahulm, *Contamination or Vaccine Research? RNA Sequencing data of early COVID-19 patient samples show abnormal presence of vectorized H7N9 hemagglutinin segment.* Abstract published July 3, 2021. Source document available at https://zenodo.org/ record/5067706#. YYQ-TkrMKUl.

Quay, Steven C. Monali C. Rahalkar, Adrian Jones, and Rahul Bahulikar, *Contamination or Vaccine Research? RNA Sequencing of Early COVID-19 Patient Samples Show Abnormal Presence of Vectorized H7N9 Hemagglutinin Segment* (2021).

Quay, Steven, MD, PhD. *Bayesian Analysis of SARS-CoV-2 Origin*, January 29, 2021, Steven@DrQuay.com.

Science Daily, November 10, 2015. *New SARS-Like Virus Can Jump Directly from Bats to Humans, No Treatment Available.* University of North Carolina at Chapel Hill. Source accessed July 6, 2021, from https://www.sciencedaily.com/ releases/2015/11/151110115711.htm.

Science Daily, November 10, 2015, University of North Carolina at Chapel Hill. Site accessed July 6, 2021 from https://www.science-daily.com/releases/2015/11/151110115711.htm.

Thomas, Liji. *The Origin of SARS-CoV-2 Furin Cleavage Site Remains a Mystery*. News Medical Life Sciences, February 17, 2021. Source accessed December 20, 2021 from https://www.news-medical.net/ news/20210217 /The-origin-of-SARS-CoV-2-furin-cleavage-site-remains-a-mystery.aspx.

GLOSSARY OF TERMS & ACRONYMS

ACE2 – An enzyme that generates proteins found on the cells of the upper and lower respiratory tracts and serves as a receptor for SARS-CoV-2 to gain access to cells and to cause infection.

BARDA – Biomedical Advanced Research Authority, an agency within HHS that develops medical countermeasure planning for vaccines and medication for public health emergencies such as CBRN incidents and pandemics.

Bayesian Analysis – a method of statistical inference in which Bayes' theorem (*see definition below*) is used to update the probability for a hypothesis as more evidence or information becomes available; specifically applied as a technique in statistical data research.

Bayes' Theorem – is used in Bayesian Analysis to describe the probability of an event based on prior knowledge of conditions that might be related to the event; the theorem expresses how a degree of probability should rationally change to account for the availability of related evidence.

Bioterrorism – in accordance with the Weapons of mass Destruction (WMD) Statute, Title 18 U.S.C. Section 2332a it is the threat or conspiracy to use a weapon of mass destruction, including any biological agent, toxin, or vector against a national of the United States or within the United States.

Biological Weapons – the weaponization of living organisms or micro-organisms or their toxic byproducts intentionally used to cause illness or death in humans, animals, or plants.

Bioinformatics – an interdisciplinary field that develops data analysis tools for interdisciplinary fields of science in biology, chemistry, physics, computer science, information engineering, mathematics, and statistics to analyze and interpret biological data.

Biowarfare – the proliferation and delivery of biological agents and viral pathogens for either military offensive or defensive weapon arsenals or the utilization of biological agents and viral pathogens for terrorist attacks against innocent civilian populations.

BMGF – Bill & Melinda Gates Foundation, a non-profit organization that is involved with the funding of globalist agenda programs to include pandemic response and COVID vaccine development.

BRI – Belt & Road Initiative also known as the "Silk Road and One Belt Road" is a global infrastructure policy developed by the Chinese government in 2013 under President Xi Jinping to expand China's economic development globally.

BSL – Biosafety Level Lab, a standard by which the environmental and safety capabilities of research laboratories are rated for their ability for biocontainment of dangerous biological agents. The BSL rating index starts with 1 as the lowest level of biosafety all the way to 4 for the highest level of containment.

B/T – acronym used in government preparedness planning and program documents for bioterrorism.

BWC – Biological Weapons Convention which represents a disarmament treaty that bans biological weapons by prohibiting their development, production, acquisition, transfer, stockpiling, and use.

CAST-USA – Chinese Association for Science and Technology, an organization that promotes collaboration between the U.S. and China for technological and scientific projects including research.

Category A Biological Agents – high priority agents that pose a risk to national security because they can be easily disseminated or transmitted from person to person causing high mortality and high morbidity.

Category B Biological Agents – agents that are moderately easy to disseminate causing moderate morbidity and low mortality.

Category C Biological Agents – agents that could be engineered for mass dissemination with the potential to for high morbidity and high mortality causing major adverse health impacts. This category includes genetically engineered or modified viral pathogens.

CBRN – Chemical, Biological, Radiological & Nuclear. The term is also applied to the response division within the Federal Emergency Management Agency that provides research and strategic planning for hazardous material containment accidents or incidents involving weapons of mass destruction.

CCP – Communist Chinese Party; the primary ruling party established by revolutionary Mao Zedong that controls and governs mainland China.

CDC – Centers for Disease Control and Prevention; federal agency under the Department of Health and Human Services headquartered in Atlanta, Georgia.

CERC – Crisis Emergency Risk Communications, planning guidance that is used to develop specific templates for press releases and protocols for working with news media through the oversight of public information officers both private and public during emergencies and pandemic response.

Chimeric Virus – a virus that contains genetic material derived from two or more distinct viruses created as a new hybrid organism (chimera) through genetic engineering.

COVID-19 – A general term for the virus based upon its acronym "CO" for corona, VI for virus, "D" for disease and the 19 representing the year it was identified.

COOP – Continuity of Operations Planning, planning directed by FEMA to establish policy and guidance for the operation of critical infrastructure in business and government during disasters and pandemics.

CPAFFC – Chinese People's Association for Friendship with Foreign Countries is organization in Beijing that promotes China's foreign affairs. This organization is a benevolent forefront to the expansion of Communist Chinese interests.

CPPCC – Chinese People's Political Consultative Conference, a delegation of high level Chinese Communist Party officials from multiple agencies to include party elders, propagandists, and military officers who plan strategic priorities for the government. This also includes representatives from the Wuhan Lab.

CRISPR – a family of DNA sequences that are utilized in viral gene editing biomedical research. Also referenced in RNA, mRNA vaccine technologies: sgRNA and Cas9 proteins.

CRT – Critical Race Theory, a radical social-justice ideology that is portrayed as a civil rights movement by activists but is influenced by Marxist philosophies of race and power in the social classes with an emphasis upon an oppressed race (systemic racism).

DARPA – Defense Advanced Research Projects Agency, a Department of Defense agency responsible for the development of emerging technologies for use by the military to include the development of COVID detection and testing systems as well providing support for nucleic acid vaccines that encode antigens. Closely aligned with DIGET (*see below*).

DHS–Department of Homeland Security, a federal agency that pro-vides oversight with national security but also has expanded roles such as climate change response and COVID vaccine operations as well as virus detection.

DIGET – Detect It with Gene Editing Technologies, an advanced research project agency for the Department of Defense that utilizes gene editing for bio surveillance, viral pathogen detection and diagnostics.

DMV – Double membrane vesicles, a distinct form of virus-induced structures found in coronaviruses as well as enteroviruses, norovi-ruses, or hepatitis C viruses.

DNA – Deoxyribonucleic Acid, a molecule composed of two polynu-cleotide chains containing basic genetic codes for all living organisms including viruses.

EcoHealth Alliance – A U.S. based non-governmental (NGO) nonprofit organization that focuses on international pandemic research and ecological conservatism. EcoHealth has been in the forefront of the gain-of-function research collaboration with Wuhan.

FDA – Food & Drug Administration, a federal agency under HHS that regulates the authorization an approval of drugs, biological products, and medical devices to include the use of vaccines.

FEMA – Federal Emergency Management Agency, the lead emergency response and planning agency for the mitigation of natural disasters. During the COVID pandemic the agency's role has been expanded significantly to include pandemic response and vaccine operations.

Global Business Network – (GBN), an international network that promotes a globalist infrastructure with a socialist agenda and is funded through the Rockefeller Foundation in partnership with venture futurist Peter Schwartz.

Global Preparedness Monitoring Board – (GPMB), created by WHO and the World Bank, an international consortium of geo-political leaders with the mission of global health security.

Global Virome Project – (GVP), an international consortium of scientists and researchers who collaborate on projects designed to identify global viral threats and to enhance pandemic preparedness capabilities through zoonotic disease surveillance. Key participants include the EcoHealth Alliance, NIH, WIV and WHO that were involved with gain-of-function research with coronaviruses in 2018.

HCD – Hydroxychloroquine; a repurposed medication used for the treatment of COVID infection that has been met with considerable resistance from large corporate pharmacies and the federal government.

HHS – The U.S. Department of Health & Human Services which administers over 100 various programs for public health nationwide and provides oversight for agencies such as the FDA and CDC.

HSEEP – Homeland Security Exercise Evaluation Program, the federal guidelines for developing and conducting emergency response drills and exercises to include after action evaluation of response capabilities and incident action plan development.

H5N1 – a highly pathogenic causative agent for avian influenza that is adapted from birds and transmitted to humans.

IAP – Incident Action Plan, a planning document that is developed after an after-action evaluation is conducted at the conclusion of a drill or exercise.

ICS – Incident Command Systems, a national framework that is used by first responders to organize emergency response.

JAMA–Journal of the American Medical Association.

Mass Prophylaxis – mass population dispensing programs for vaccines and medical countermeasures.

MERS – Middle Eastern Respiratory Syndrome, a viral respiratory illness of recent origins first identified in Saudi Arabia in 2012. MERS is of the same genus as SARS-CoV-2.

MOOTW – Military Operations Other Than War is a strategic plan of the People's Liberation Army of China to utilize technologically elite modern weapons that have the capability to attack an enemy from a place beyond his range. These are usually non-conventional weapons which include anything from cyber warfare viruses to genetically engineered viruses capable of mass destruction.

mRNA – Messenger RNA vaccine technology that specifically codes proteins to activate an immune response to the COVID-19 virus.

NACCHO – National Association of County & City Health Officials, an organization based in Washington, D.C. t hat is a network for local, city, county, and district public health departments that provides guidance for public health infrastructure to include pandemic preparedness, climate change planning, and social health equity programs.

NATO – North Atlantic Treaty Organization also referred to as the North Atlantic Alliance established in 1949 that is an international military alliance between 27 European countries, 2 North American countries and 1 Eurasian country.

NIAID – National Institute of Allergy & Infectious Diseases, an agency within the NIH and HHS that conducts and supports clinical trials for COVID vaccines and conducts applied research regarding infectious diseases.

NIH – National Institutes of Health; medical research center that is an agency of the federal health and human services that has been involved with gain-of-function research collaboration.

Nipah Virus – a bat-borne virus common in Asian countries which is lethal and has a high infection and morbidity rate; Nipah virus is recognized as a category C Biological Agent that is capable of being genetically engineered as a bioweapon as it is a compatible candidate for pairing with SARS-CoV-2 spiked protein clusters. Nipah virus was discovered in cross-contaminated samples from the Wuhan Lab.

NCCDPHP – National Center for Chronic Disease Prevention & Health Promotion, an agency under the CDC that promotes a public health social equity platform.

NPI – Non-pharmaceutical Interventions, response planning for isolation and quarantine enforcement during pandemics.

NRF – National Response Framework, the federal coordination system for emergency planning.

NSABB – National Science Advisory Board, a federal advisory committee chartered to provide advice, guidance, and recommendations to the U.S. government regarding biosecurity oversight of dual use research and gain-of-function research.

OSHA – Occupational Safety & Health Administration, a federal regulatory agency within the US Department of Labor.

Pathogen – a specific causative agent for infectious disease that is either viral or bacterial.

PAPR – Powered Air Purifying Respirators, consisting of air purifying self-contained respirators combined with a helmet or hood that is commonly used in BSL-3 or BSL-4 environments where personnel are exposed to highly lethal pathogens.

Phenotype – the set of observable characteristics or traits of an organism that also includes morphology or structure and its developmental processes and properties.

Phylogenetic Analysis – the study of the evolutionary development of a species or a group of organisms. This analysis can be specifically applied to gain-of-function research to further understand the viral organisms which are genetically modified or engineered.

PIO – Public Information Officer or public information office, the agency or department that oversees the development of press releases and social media for private corporations as well as government agencies during an emergency or a pandemic (*also see CERC*).

PLA – People's Liberation Army; the armed forces of the Communist People's Republic of China which consists of China's Ground Force, Navy, Air Force, Rocket Force and Strategic Support Force.

PPE – Personal Protective Equipment which includes items such as respirators, gowns, boots, gloves, and faces shields, necessary for the appropriate level of safety for personnel within specific sterilized medical or laboratory environments.

PPP – Potential Pandemic Pathogen that is highly transmissible and likely to have uncontrolled spread in local populations.

PRC – People's Republic of China; general designation used for the nation of mainland China.

PREDICT Project – an international global zoonotic viral surveillance project with the aim to detect and discover viruses that have pandemic potential. PREDICT is funded by USAID as part of their Emerging Pandemic Threats Program which also partners with EcoHealth Alliance, UC Davis (University of California), and the Smithsonian Institution.

RaTG13 – a coronavirus found in horseshoe bats which was first discovered by Wuhan Lab researchers in 2013 when miners in Yunnan

China were infected from bat fecal matter. This is the closest known viral pathogen source for SARS-CoV-2 that caused the COVID-19 pandemic. The WIV did extensive research on RaTG13 several years prior to the pandemic.

Recombinant Virus – when a virus can be produced by either natural recombining of DNA or through synthetic means such as in the production of vaccines by using genetically engineered viruses.

RGS – Reverse Genetics System (*see full definition below*).

Reverse Genetics System – a method in molecular genetics that is used to study the gain of function of a gene by analyzing the phenotype effects caused by a genetically engineered nucleic acid sequence within the gene.

RNA – Ribonucleic Acid, a polymeric molecule essential in various biological roles for coding and decoding for lipids, proteins, carbohydrates, and nucleic acids that are essential in all living organisms.

SARS – Severe Acute Respiratory Syndrome, a viral respiratory disease of zoonotic (animal) origin. SARS is the first identified strain of SARS-CoV as it is of the same genus.

SARS-CoV-2 – one of the four subclassifications of coronaviruses found in bats and rodents known as betacoronaviruses also known as severe acute respiratory syndrome coronavirus 2 which is the cause of the COVID-19 pandemic.

SHC014-CoV – a SARS like virus found in horseshoe bats that can jump between bats and humans that can replicate in human lung cells like SARS-CoV and was studied closely by the Wuhan Lab prior to the pandemic.

SITMAN – Situation Manual, utilized as the primary planning tool for exercises and drills to include simulated scenarios for pandemic response and other emergency incidents.

SNS – Strategic National Stockpile, a federal repository within the domain of HHS and CDC for vaccines, medical equipment established to provide medical countermeasures during a pandemic or biological attack. SNS planning and coordination is pushed out to all local and state health departments.

U.N. – United Nations, a globalist organization which promotes socialist agendas and provides oversight for the WHO.

UNC–University of North Carolina; primary participant in gain-of-function research with Wuhan Lab.

USAMRIID – U.S. Army Medical Research Institute of Infectious Diseases, established at Fort Detrick, Maryland which specializes in bioweapons research.

USSR – Soviet Union of Socialist Republics, a Russian sovereign Communist state of Soviet Republics also known as the Soviet Union that existed from 1922 to 1991; the largest developer of biological weapons next to China.

WHO–World Health Organization; specialized agency of the United Nations responsible for international public health within a globalist/socialist framework.

WIV – Wuhan Institute of Virology which leads viral research in China and is "ground-zero" for COVID-19.

WIBP – Wuhan Institute of Biological Products, a facility adjacent to the WIV that has been involved with the research and development of COVID vaccines.

WMD – Weapons of Mass Destruction that include the proliferation and delivery of chemical, biological, radiological, and nuclear (CBRN) weapons as defined by NATO.

Zoonotic – an infectious disease originating in animals caused by a viral pathogen that can infect humans.

9 781662 848797